The
TEACHER'S
CRAFT

The
TEACHER'S
CRAFT

The 10 Essential Skills of
Effective Teaching

Paul Chance

WAVELAND

PRESS, INC.

Long Grove, Illinois

For information about this book, contact:
Waveland Press, Inc.
4180 IL Route 83, Suite 101
Long Grove, IL 60047-9580
(847) 634-0081
info@waveland.com
www.waveland.com

10-digit ISBN 1-57766-559-7
13-digit ISBN 978-1-57766-559-5

Printed in the United States of America

7   6   5   4   3   2   1

For

Thomas E. Chance,

one of my best teachers

Contents

Preface

There are any number of books on teaching. Most of them were written by former teachers and offer pearls of wisdom gleaned from their personal experience in the classroom. This is not that sort of book.

Yes, I have taught. I have taught grades 7, 8, and 9 in regular public schools; I have taught high school dropouts in an alternative school; middle-aged adults working for Black and Decker or Perdue Farms and preparing to take the GED; community college students taking courses in English; and university students taking psychology. I even taught basic computer skills to elementary school children as a volunteer in a public library. But this book is not an autobiographical account of my experiences, nor is it the distillation of hard-earned wisdom. This book is an effort to offer what the best available evidence says about effective teaching.

I started with the assumption that teaching is a craft, an occupation requiring knowledge and expertise that can be acquired through study and practice. As obvious as that may seem, it is widely disputed.

So far as I know, no case of educational malpractice brought against a teacher or school has ever been decided in favor of the plaintiff. The reason is that in order to rule that someone is guilty of malpractice, there has to be a recognized standard of what *good* practice is. You can win a suit against a doctor or hospital for malpractice because there is a widely accepted notion within medicine of what constitutes good medical practice. In education, the courts have said, there is no agreement about what constitutes good educational practice.

This book is an attempt to show that there *is* a body of knowledge about what constitutes good educational practice. It attempts to show that teaching is a craft.

The Teacher's Craft is intended for anyone contemplating teaching: college students preparing to teach, new teachers who are struggling to find their way, home schoolers who realize that being a parent doesn't necessarily make you a teacher, and experienced teachers eager to hone their skills.

In making the case for the notion of a teacher's craft, I have limited myself to well-documented (but frequently neglected or denied) principles. There is nothing to be found in these pages on brain-based teaching (the current fad) or wisdom training (the likely fad of tomorrow). I have made the book as brief as possible so that you will come away from it enlightened rather than confused. I have tried to write a book that is easy and fun to read so that you *will* read it, perhaps more than once. But most of all I have tried to show that the case for the ten essential skills described here is so compelling that even though your present views may be quite different, you may say upon completing the book, "I already knew most of this stuff."

And that will be fine with me. I *want* you to own these ideas, to feel in your bones that they are obvious, intuitive, common sense. For that will mean you have taken an important step toward developing your skill at the teacher's craft.

Acknowledgments

Every book is a group project. The author produces a manuscript, but lots of other people are needed to turn that manuscript into a book. I am grateful to Neil Rowe, Publisher of Waveland Press, for believing in the project from the start. My heartfelt thanks go to everyone on the Waveland team: to Gayle Zawilla, who deftly edited the manuscript and found the cartoons we needed to make my words memorable; to Jan Weissman, for obtaining the related permissions; to Deborah Underwood, for her illustrations and photo editing; to Katy Murphy, for her interior design and typesetting; and to Don Rosso, for his willingness to work with me on the cover design. Writers always say that small presses are the best to work with, and it's true. Working with Waveland has been the best book publishing experience I've had.

I also want to thank those who offered information and moral support as I prepared the manuscript: Judy Cameron of the University of Alberta; Robert Eisenberger of the University of Delaware; Bill Hopkins, Emeritus Professor at Auburn University; Kent Johnson of Morningside Academy; Henry Schlinger of California State University, Los Angeles; Howard Sloane, Emeritus Professor at the University of Utah; and Tim Slocum of Utah State University. I am grateful to my good friend Brian Weiss of Wordsworth for his constant support and his many helpful suggestions. I hope I have not left anyone out, but if I have I offer my sincere apologies.

Prologue
What Is Teaching?

> *Teaching makes learning happen.*
> —Wesley Becker

An outstanding teacher makes all the difference in the world. One of the things we know for sure about education is that there is nothing anyone can do to improve student achievement that is as important as providing highly skilled teachers. Nothing.

All sorts of evidence support this statement, but the best may be studies comparing the progress of students who were lucky enough to get good teachers with those who were unfortunate enough to get bad ones.[1]

William Sanders, former director of the Value-Added Research and Assessment Center at the University of Tennessee, has led the way in this area.* Year after year he measured the academic progress of Tennessee's school children. Taking into account IQ, socioeconomic status, past achievement, and other factors, Sanders estimated how much each student could be expected to learn, as measured by standardized achievement tests. By comparing expected performance with the student's actual achievement, Sanders was able to gauge the effectiveness of individual teachers. He found that some teachers got markedly better results than would be expected, given the characteristics of their students, whereas other teachers got substantially worse results than would be expected.

For instance, in one study Sanders and J. C. Rivers compared the math skills of fifth graders who had been assigned to either very effective or very ineffective teachers for three years in two school systems.[2] In one school system the students with the best teachers scored at the 83rd percentile, while those with the worst teachers scored at the 29th percentile. In the second school system, students with the best teachers scored at the 96th percentile; those with the worst scored at the 44th percentile. In each case, the assignment of teachers made a difference in average scores of more than 50 percentile points!

Other studies tell a similar story. H. R. Jordan and colleagues, for example, looked at reading and math scores after three years with both very good and very poor teachers.[3] Students who had very effective teachers scored at the 76th percentile in both reading and math, while those who had ineffective teachers scored at the 42nd and 27th percentiles in reading and math, respectively.

It is truly remarkable how much difference a single teacher can make in a student's progress. Sanders has found that it may take a student *four years* to recover from the effects of *one* year with an ineffective teacher.[4] The student who gets poor teachers for three consecutive years may *never* fully recover, even if he or she then gets excellent teachers.

And it isn't just the weakest students who benefit from stellar teaching. Kati Haycock, director of the Education Trust, notes that good teachers produce markedly better results in students regardless of their previous achievements. In other words, good teaching benefits *all* students.[5]

So, forget about race, parental education, family income, ethnic background, the sequence of courses in the curriculum, the number of computers in the school, class size, school uniforms, outdated textbooks, the number of vacation days, and anything else you've heard about that might affect student learning. The elephant in the room is *how teachers teach*. The quality of teaching is not only the most important factor in student learning, it is so far out in front that it doesn't even matter what comes in second.[6]

---

*Unless otherwise noted, researchers mentioned are either educational researchers or educational psychologists.

But what, exactly, does teaching mean? There are lots of answers to that question, but rather than review them here I will simply offer my own:

*Teaching means doing things that improve the
rate, durability, and transfer of learning.*

At the risk of being referred to a support group for obsessive-compulsive writers, I will discuss this definition in some detail. This is, after all, a book about teaching, so we should start off with a clear understanding of what I mean by the term.

It may be best to begin the discussion with the word *learning*. People typically think of learning as the process of storing something inside one's head, invisible to the outside world. In some sense what is learned *is* stored inside the person, but it doesn't do much good there. Accordingly, we can say that students have learned only if they can do something now that they couldn't do before, or if they can do it better than they did before. For instance:

- A four-year-old who could not count past five now counts to ten; a classmate who could count to ten, but slowly and hesitantly, now rattles off the numbers with ease.
- An eleven-year-old who had never heard the word *logic* is now a master of the syllogism and can prove in an instant that Socrates was mortal, even without seeing his death certificate.
- A sixteen-year-old who could not tell a right triangle from a slice of pizza now can identify a dozen geometric forms, from an isosceles triangle to a dodecahedron.
- A fifty-two-year-old truck driver who could read only a handful of traffic signs now reads a daily newspaper.

We may think of learning as storing things away in our heads, but generally it must come out into the open to be of value. To know is to be capable of action.

The word *rate* means change over time. If you want to get mathematical about it, learning rate can be defined as the amount learned (the number of geometric forms that can be identified, for example) divided by the number of minutes or hours spent learning.

Concepts like learning rate are annoying to some people because, they argue, many of the most important things students learn do not fit neatly into the little boxes that educational researchers like to check off. A student who is no longer terrified to speak before a class has learned something very important, but it is not easy to express that learning in educational units.

Nevertheless, we cannot escape the importance of rate in our definition of teaching. For example, two teachers work with similar five-year-olds for an hour a day, attempting to teach them to read. At the end of the school year, one student is reading *Charlotte's Web* and the other can't read a stop sign. More than any other single variable, the rate at which children learn defines the quality of teaching that is occurring. Like it or not, common sense dictates that the rate of learning matters.

So does the *durability* of learning. Somebody wryly noted that most college students remember little from their study of the American Civil War except that the South wore gray and the North wore blue. Studies of the retention of school learning consistently show an appalling rate of forgetting. Many students who study a foreign language, for instance, forget what they learned so quickly that within a few years they are scarcely better off than those who never studied the language at all.[7]

It is possible, of course, to justify teaching things that we know students will forget. The study of mathematics might have long-term beneficial effects on a student's problem-solving skills. The study of a foreign language might increase a student's willingness to struggle doggedly with difficult tasks and to embrace people from other cultures. The study of history can give the student an understanding of the way in which events are shaped by economical, political, and scientific developments. But the fact that students may benefit from learning something, even if they later forget it, does not mean that forgetting it is a good thing. If something is worth learning, it is also worth remembering. Hence, improving student retention of what they learn is an important part of teaching.

Teaching means improving *transfer*. Transfer is the tendency of learning to carry over from one situation to another. Teachers generally assume that transfer is automatic. During a grammar lesson, teach a student the difference between fragments and complete sentences, and when she writes an essay for a science lesson, she will no longer write in fragments. But in fact what students learn in one situation typically does *not* automatically carry over to other settings. It may not even carry over within the same classroom. A professor at a prestigious university once said that he taught students in a statistics class about normal distribution (the bell curve) using weight as an example. He noted that if you weighed a number of people, you would find that some would be very heavy, some would be very thin, and most would be somewhere in between. He then showed them that if you plotted the results on a graph, you would get something like a bell-shaped curve. The lesson went well and the students seem to "get it." The next day, the instructor asked the students to plot a hypothetical graph of the bell curve for height. He was astonished to find that most students couldn't do it. What they learned about plotting the curve for weight did not transfer to plotting the curve for height.

Even reading does not automatically transfer outside the classroom. Students who read a basal reader smoothly in school may stumble when reading a library book on the same reading level at home. Even more importantly, the tendency to read when directed to do so by a teacher in school may not result in the tendency to read at home when no teacher is around. Yet surely we want students who not only *can* read when asked to, but who *choose* to read even when nobody is asking.

Finally, teaching means *doing things*. The difference between good teachers and bad ones is a matter of what they *do* in the classroom. This should be obvious, but apparently it is not. Ask school principals, "What makes for a good teacher?" and many point to personality characteristics and physical appearance, not to how teachers teach. The research evidence, however, consistently shows that what most distinguishes highly effective teachers from their less successful colleagues is what they do in the classroom.[8]

What do the best teachers do that the weakest teachers don't? In attempting to answer this question I have studied both outstanding teachers and educational research.

Teachers who have gained fame (or notoriety) for excellent results offer hints about good teaching. Consider, for example, Jaime Escalante, the Bolivian immigrant who for many years taught mathematics at James A. Garfield High School in East Los Angeles and was made famous by the film, *Stand and Deliver*. Garfield is in a low-income Hispanic neighborhood where about 80% of students qualify for free or reduced lunch.

Prior to Escalante's arrival in 1976, no Garfield student had ever taken the advanced placement (AP) test in calculus. Escalante taught his first calculus class in 1979. He had five students, two of whom passed the AP test that year. By 1981, 15 students took the class and 14 passed the exam. A year later, Escalante gained national attention when 18 students passed the test, a result so extraordinary for an urban school in a low-income area that the Educational Testing Service (ETS), publisher of the AP tests, suspected the students of cheating. ETS asked 14 of the students to re-take the exam; 12 did, and all had their scores reinstated. In 1983, 33 of Escalante's students took the test and 30 passed. In 1987, 73 Garfield students passed the basic AP test, and another 12 passed a more difficult version of the test usually reserved for second-year calculus students.

A few years later, Escalante and fellow math teacher Ben Jimenez left Garfield because of conflicts with a newly installed principal. Over the next few years, the number of Garfield students passing the AP calculus exam fell like a skydiver in free fall.[9]

Highly effective teachers, such as Escalante in California, Marva Collins in Chicago, Reuven Feuerstein in Israel, and others, offer clues about successful teaching, and their methods should be studied.[10] I do not suggest that these teachers are miracle workers or that everything they do is right. Escalante, for example, once gathered up all of Garfield's band uniforms and musical instruments and threw them into a dumpster. He objected to band, art classes, and anything else that might tempt students away from the study of mathematics.

Most people, I think, would say that there is value in learning to play a musical instrument or appreciate art, even if the time devoted to these activities means learning a little less about mathematics. But while Escalante and other famous teachers may not be ideal models, the success of their students suggests that they got some things right. It makes sense to try to learn what those things are.

There is also a huge body of research (about 40,000 studies according to one account) on various forms of instruction.[11] Some of this research provides clear and consistent evidence of the components of effective teaching.

For example, in 1968, Robert Rosenthal and Lenore Jacobson reported research on the effects of teacher expectations on student learning.[12] In these experiments, the researchers led teachers to believe that certain students in their classes would make exceptional progress. These students were in no way superior to their peers and were, in fact, selected at random. Despite this, the researchers discovered that the "special" students learned more than their peers. Their teachers' expectations had become a self-fulfilling prophecy.[13] Rosenthal called the phenomenon the Pygmalion effect, after the story of the statue brought to life by the love of the sculptor who created it.

Largely as a result of these classic experiments, many educators now often speak of the importance of having high expectations. "You have to believe your students can do it," they suggest, "in order for them to do it." This has been called the Tinker Bell effect, after the fairy in *Peter Pan*. Fairies exist, Tinker Bell said, only if people believe they exist! In the same way, many teachers believe that their students can do wonderful things, as long as the teachers believe they can! But in fact there is no evidence that teacher expectations, as such, have any effect whatever on student learning. No one has ever shown, for example, that a student reading a book in one room learned more if a teacher sitting in another room had high expectations for the student. The effect of expectations is indirect. When teachers expect good things from a student, they teach differently.

Rosenthal examined a number of Pygmalion studies and found that expectations changed teacher behavior in four ways. Teachers who expected students to do well (1) covered more material (e.g., gave students more spelling words to learn, discussed historical events in more detail); (2) required students to perform more often (e.g., called on them more often); (3) provided more feedback (e.g., told them when they got something right, answered their questions more fully); and (4) treated the students more warmly (e.g., touched them, made eye contact, smiled at them more). It is these changes in teacher *behavior*, said Rosenthal, not some telepathic transmission of expectations, that produces greater student learning.[14] Educational research of this sort has clear implications for teaching.

The point is that there is much to learn from a study of good teachers and good research. I have attempted to sift through this material in search of recurring themes. I have paid little attention to teaching strategies that seem idiosyncratic or to research findings that are "statistically significant" but of no practical value. The goal has been to identify things any teacher can do that will make a substantial difference in how much his or her students learn.

This is not to say that anyone who reads this book will then automatically teach well. Reading about effective teaching is one thing; teaching effectively is something else again. A study by Kent Johnson and Joe Layng of Morningside Academy will illustrate.

Morningside Academy is a private remedial school in Seattle. It is also a place where teachers can go to learn the "Morningside Model" in summer workshops. These are not the usual weekend workshops in which teachers listen to four hours of lectures while enjoying coffee and donuts. The Morningside workshops are 100 hours of intense instruction and practice in the use of the Morningside methods. Johnson and Layng found that teachers who had this training were highly effective and got the same results as the Morningside teachers.

But is 100 hours of instruction really necessary? What would happen, Johnson and Layng wondered, if they cut the training program in half? The concepts were not difficult to grasp, so maybe 50 hours would be enough, and twice as many teachers could be trained in the same time. Johnson and Layng did the experiment. They found that students learned only half as much from teachers who received 50 hours of training as they did from teachers who received 100 hours of training.[15] Teachers are made, not born, and it takes time and hard work to make the best ones.

So I make no claim that reading this book will, in itself, turn you into a highly effective teacher. My goal is far more modest: to let you know what the evidence suggests are the most important elements of effective teaching.

The combination of these elements forms an approach to teaching that has no particular name. It is most definitely *not* the Chance model. My role has been merely to pull together information others have provided, and to present it in a succinct and readable form. If you must give this approach a name, call it deliberate teaching, active teaching, explicit teaching, purposeful teaching, or guided teaching. Or just call it teaching.[16]

Call it what you will, it is a set of skills that together markedly improve student performance. With a knowledge of these skills, the guidance of competent teachers, and feedback from your own students, you may one day become a good teacher. You might even become one of those outstanding teachers who make all the difference in the world.

1

Create a Learning Climate

Cheerfulness is the atmosphere in which all things thrive.
—Jean Paul Richter

Walk down the halls of almost any school and peer into the class-rooms and you will find that each room has its own special microclimate. Over here, the skies are gray, it is raining buckets, there's a chill in the air, and everyone is in a dark mood and eager to leave. Across the hall, the sun is shining, there's a warm breeze, birds are singing, and everyone is cheerful and glad to be where they are.

The atmosphere of a classroom is a powerful influence on the progress students make.[1] But why does the climate differ so much from one classroom to another? Some say the difference is a matter of luck. Groups of students differ, just as individual students do, and the differences in atmosphere reflect these differences. "I'd like to see Mrs. Howard take *my* class," they say, "and see what sort of atmosphere she has with those imps!"

I don't buy it. Sure, some groups of students are harder to work with than others. But when one teacher has cheerful, hard-working students year after year and another teacher has grumpy slackers again and again, I have to think something besides luck is involved. That something else is teacher behavior: Teachers do certain things that shape the climate for good or ill.

How does a teacher create a climate conducive to learning? Regrettably, there is no surefire formula for establishing a great learning climate. But research, everyday experience, and common sense do provide certain clues about things teachers can do to improve the atmosphere in their part of the world.

Provide an environment that is safe, attractive, and comfortable. Teachers are enjoined to act *in loco parentis*, Latin for *in the place of the parent*. The phrase means that the teacher is responsible for doing the kinds of things that the best parents would do in similar circumstances to protect a child's well-being. It is what I call the Prime Directive of education: Let no harm come to your students.[2]

Fortunately, American schools are generally free from serious violence, and most students are at least as safe in school as they are in their own homes.[3] A survey of teachers by Public Agenda suggested that most teachers are not particularly concerned about serious problems such as drugs and guns in school. Rather, the concern is about relatively minor aggravations such as horseplay and disrespect.[4]

Sometimes there are, however, hazardous conditions in schools: Lead-tainted paint peels from the wall, tiles fall from the ceiling, electrical outlets lack covers, water puddles on the floor when it rains, toilets back up.[5] You cannot be expected to correct major safety hazards, but you can and should take appropriate action. At the very least, you should provide your principal and the maintenance staff with a written list of safety hazards in your room. If this gets no results, you might invite some parents to come in to see the hazards and suggest that they contact the authorities. You can also chat about the problem with your friend, the reporter.[6]

Even if these efforts fail, they will at least provide you with some protection from litigation if a child is injured. If you do not notify the authorities of the hazards, you can be sure they will say the fault is yours. ("We would have filled the sinkhole in the middle of the floor immediately if only Ms. Jones had informed us of the problem—which, of course, we knew nothing about.")

Activism on behalf of students can be personally costly, which is why many teachers do nothing. Principals, school-board members, and superintendents have been known to retaliate against teachers who make waves, even when they do so on behalf of their students. But part of your job is to follow the Prime Directive, even when this brings you into conflict with those who are more concerned about maintaining the status quo than about protecting students.

Structural flaws are not the only kinds of safety hazards in schools. Bullies threaten, manhandle, and rob weaker students in the halls, in the washrooms, on the playground, and even in classrooms. The potential victims have only the teacher to turn to for protection. Some teachers turn a blind eye, and that deliberate blindness undermines the quality of the learning environment. How well could *you* concentrate on the multiplication tables if you knew that at the end of the period Max would take your lunch money and grind your face into the dirt? Kids know that survival is more important than arithmetic.

It helps to know that bullies are typically academically weak and unpopular students. Bullying is not just a way of getting someone else's lunch money. It's a way of obtaining status and influence by students who would otherwise have neither. Bullies can benefit from academic tutoring and instruction in basic social skills; as they improve, so will the classroom climate.

Safety is a minimal requirement for every classroom. To have a climate conducive to learning, the classroom should also be attractive and comfortable. Burned-out ceiling lights may not pose a physical hazard, but they literally make for a gloomy environment. Dirty floors, graffiti-covered walls, broken windows, wobbly furniture, worn-out books, a heating system that provides only two temperatures (too hot and too cold)—all of these things undermine learning.[7]

The physical features of a classroom, and of a school in general, convey to students very clearly what value the responsible adults place on their education. The steady plop, plop, plop of water falling into a bucket on a rainy day tells the student that the community cares not, not, not about their education. The teacher who makes an effort to improve the physical condition of her classroom proves that she, at least, cares.

You may not be able to renovate the school, but you can do a lot to improve the appearance of your room. Teachers often decorate the walls with colorful posters related to the subjects they teach. Posters can often be obtained for free or for next to nothing from businesses that produce them for advertising purposes. Children's book publishers, for instance, often produce posters to display their books in bookstores. The publisher or stores might be delighted to provide them free to teachers for classroom use. Bright, cheery posters illustrating scenes from age-appropriate films also make a room more attractive and interesting. Ask your local movie theater if you can have the lobby posters when they're through with them.

Another decorating idea is to prepare banners with quotations from historical figures, artists, musicians, novelists, scientists, athletes, and that most prolific of writers, Anonymous, and post them on the walls near the ceiling.

One idea is to have a set of quotations around some theme, such as famous last words. George Washington's "It is well. I die hard, but I am not afraid to go" and Nathan Hale's "My only regret is that I have but one life to give for my country" are bound to be popular. Pearls of wisdom from athletes are also good. One example is champion runner Florence Griffith Joyner's "Nothing is going to be handed to you. You have to make things happen."

Each time a new poster or quotation goes up, draw attention to it, have a short discussion, and refer to it from time to time. This will help to make the banners both attractive and instructional. Most wall decorations shouldn't remain up throughout the school year but should be replaced from time to time.

You might enrich the value of these decorations by encouraging students to bring in quotations they have come across in their reading or elsewhere. Many of their suggested quotations will come from sources such as the Harry Potter books or popular movies. The quotes may be less than profound, but anything you can do to get students to "own" the classroom, to see it as *their* space for learning, is worthwhile.

Try putting up a quotation from a student who says something interesting in a paper or during a class discussion. Imagine the surprise and pleasure of a student, whether in kindergarten or high school, at walking into a room and seeing his or her own words alongside those of George Washington and Martin Luther King, Jr.

An obvious thing that all teachers can do to improve the attractiveness of a room is to keep it clean and neat. In doing so, the teacher conveys not only an important value, but also the regard in which he holds his students.

"I'm your teacher, Mrs. Gridley. Learn to read, write, and do arithmetic, and nobody will get hurt."

© Stan Fine

Students deserve and need to be reasonably comfortable. That means, for example, that they have chairs to sit on, and that the chairs are in good condition and suitable for their size. If good chairs are in short supply, you can do the right thing and submit a request (in triplicate) through the proper channels, in which case you might get chairs at the end of the year—possibly the year you qualify for social security. Or, you can wander the halls after hours looking for chairs you can rescue from a lifetime of neglect. Sometimes you'll find them stuffed away in the back of storage closets, waiting patiently for deliverance. Once you have good chairs, you might want to write your room number on the seat bottoms with indelible ink, in case they wander off.

Let your students know what is expected of them. A good way to get the kind of behavior you want from students is to let them know what that behavior is. Many teachers attempt to do this by compiling long lists of rules, often writing them on the board. Usually these are DON'T rules: Don't call out answers. Don't run indoors. Don't shout. Don't litter. Don't chew gum. Don't walk on my desk. . . .

The trouble is that there are so many things students should *not* do that you can't possibly list them all. ("I'm not chewing gum; I'm chewing betel nuts." "I wasn't running; I was skipping.") You fall into a "you and them" relationship—teacher as cop, student as criminal. A better practice is to compose a short list (no more than a dozen) of DO rules, such as:

- Raise your hand to speak.
- Walk when indoors.
- Speak quietly.
- Clean up your area before leaving the room.
- Hang your coat in the closet.

These rules would establish how the daily routines, such as participating in class discussions, getting to and from the library and cafeteria, dismissal, and so on, are to be handled.

Some teachers post a large display of the Golden Rule: "Treat others as you would like to be treated." The Golden Rule must, of course, get translated into concrete practice, but this can be done in the context of daily situations rather than in the abstract form of a list of commandments. "Billy, shoving is not acceptable. I'm sure you don't like to be shoved by others." Whenever possible, the emphasis should be on what students should do (speak quietly) rather than on what they should not do (don't shout).

You can give some flesh and blood to the Golden Rule by making a very short speech, for example:

> We don't know each other yet, but I'm sure we'll get along well. But there's one thing you need to know about me right from the start: I can't stand and won't tolerate meanness—doing things that hurt other people. Not just hitting, pinching, or shoving people, but teasing, threatening, calling them names, and lots of other things. When you come into this room, I want you to feel safe. I want you to know that I will not make fun of you or say hurtful things to you or about you. And I will not tolerate that kind of behavior from others.

The Golden Rule doesn't cover everything, so some routine activities will have to be governed by other rules. These rules are best taught incidentally, as the need arises. For instance, if you want students to wait for you to dismiss them, let them know this shortly before the bell rings: "The bell will ring in a moment, and when it does I want you to gather up your things and wait quietly for me to dismiss you." Similarly, before the lunch bell, you might say, "When the lunch bell rings, I want you to line up at the back door in two lines, then wait for me to open the door." It won't be long before they know exactly how to go about the routines of school life. Failure to establish these kinds of routines, especially in the elementary grades, will mean disorderly behavior that will inevitably steal time from learning activities.

Live up to your students' expectations. Teachers have expectations for students, but they aren't always aware that students have expectations for teachers. Yet when teachers fail to meet student expectations, the learning climate suffers.

One thing students expect is that the teacher will be prepared to teach. The teacher who can't find a piece of chalk to write on the board, who struggles to read his messy lesson notes, who spends 30 seconds rooting through a folder for the right handout, whose slides are in the wrong order in the projector, who gives a reading assignment the students have already done, who stumbles through a PowerPoint presentation because he hasn't mastered the software, who begins a lesson with, "Where did we leave off yesterday?" will quickly lose the respect and admiration of his students. He will also find his students coming to class unprepared, and when neither teacher nor students are prepared not much learning takes place.

Students expect a teacher to meet or exceed the standards for conduct she sets for *them*. It is absurd, for example, for a teacher to shout, "Don't shout!" And teachers who are mean will have students who are mean. Master teacher Marva Collins notes that "children are quick to mimic adults. If a teacher ridicules or picks on a child, chances are the children will pick on each other."[8] If the students are to follow the Golden Rule, the teacher must try to provide a golden model.

Students expect teachers to enforce their rules. Teachers often do just the opposite. Many teachers want students to raise their hands and wait to be called on rather than call out answers. They recognize that if students call out, the shyer and slower students never get a chance to answer. Yet when a student calls out a correct answer, some teachers say, "Yes, that's correct," and continue the lesson. The student who disobeys the rule is recognized, while those who raise their hands are ignored. If calling out works, that is what students will do, regardless of the rules. Classroom rules mean nothing if the teacher doesn't follow them.[9]

Students expect teachers to act like adults. Some teachers try to be the students' pal. They have been known to tell students about their personal problems—they're getting divorced, they have a lot of credit card debt, they're not getting along with the principal. Students want teachers to care about them, to look out for them, to treat them with respect, but they want them to be grown-ups, not pals.

One way the teacher conveys that she is an adult is by the way she dresses. Although there isn't a lot of research on the sartorial habits of teachers, there is some evidence that how teachers dress affects the way students behave. Pamela Phillips and Lyle Smith found, for example, that students perceive casually dressed teachers as friendly but view conservatively dressed teachers as knowledgeable and good disciplinarians.[10] And it seems likely that there is a link between teacher attire and student conduct.[11]

It used to be standard practice for male teachers to wear jacket and tie and for women to wear dresses or pantsuits. Today, casual dress is the uniform of the day, and in many high schools it is difficult to distinguish between the oldest students and the youngest teachers because they dress the same. If you really want students to think of you as "one of the guys," dress as they do—complete with tight-fitting jeans, orange hair, calf tattoo, and pierced nose. You are sure to be considered the coolest teacher in school. On the other hand, if you want students to think of you as a professional, and the classroom as a place where important work is done, you probably should dress like an adult.

Follow the Rule of Eight. It may well be that nothing so influences the climate of a classroom as the emotional tone of communications from the teacher to students. Teachers who yell at students, call them names, strike or shake them, or threaten to do so are establishing poor conditions for learning. Most teachers know this, of course, including those who do these things. But many teachers are unaware how often they do more subtle things that make for a demoralizing atmosphere.

This point is supported by the work of the late Glenn Latham, educational consultant and director of the Mountain Plains Regional Research Center at Utah State University. Latham spent hundreds of hours observing teachers at work. During these observations he usually counted the number of positive and negative comments a teacher made. If the teacher said, "Phyllis, get rid of that gum!" Latham counted that as one negative comment. If the teacher said, "That's a good question," Latham counted that as a positive comment.

Latham tallied the positive and negative comments and then calculated the ratio between them. Typically, in classrooms all over the country, he found that the number of negatives was greater than the number of positives, usually by a ratio of at least two to one. Other researchers have gotten similar results. Charles Madsen found, for example, that 77% of the interactions between elementary school teachers and their students were negative, a ratio of three to one.[12] In some classes, negative teacher comments outnumber positive ones by 15 to 1! Moreover, some students *never* hear a positive comment, even when they do good work and comply with teacher requests. Nor is the phenomenon restricted to American teachers. Robyn Beaman and Kevin Wheldall reviewed the literature on teacher comments in the United States, Canada, the United Kingdom, Australia, New Zealand, and Hong Kong and concluded that teachers in all of these places were far more likely to comment negatively on inappropriate behavior than they were to comment positively on appropriate behavior.[13]

You may be thinking, "Well, duh! The teachers make negative comments because the students aren't doing their work. If students misbehave a lot, the number of negative comments has to be higher than the number of positive comments. The teacher has no choice."

But she does. Teachers can give negative attention to the student who is staring out of the window, or she can give positive attention to the student who is focused on his work. If she elects to do the former, the mood of the room shifts to the negative; if she chooses to do the latter, the mood shifts to the positive. The direction of this shift can have a profound effect on student performance.[14]

At one school with a great many "high-risk" (i.e., poor, minority) students, *80%* of the students were assigned to special education classes. School administrators asked Glenn Latham if he could do something to lower that figure. After observing classes and recording positive and negative teacher comments, he discovered that the ratio of positive to negative statements was about 1 to 4. (That is, teachers and aides made one positive comment for every four negative comments.) Latham taught the teachers to focus on the positive and got the ratio up to more than 40 to 1—40 positive statements for every negative one. What effect did the new ratio have on students? The following year, only 11% of students were placed in special education classes, compared to 80% the year before.[15]

As Latham writes, "Teachers have simply *got* to learn to be *much* more positive and encouraging than negative and discouraging."[16] Over the years, he found that if teachers provide at least eight positive comments for every negative one, the result is almost always a harmonious classroom in which students learn a lot. Latham began to speak of the Rule of Eight, and he believed that following this rule might be the single most important thing teachers can do to improve classroom climate and enhance the rate of learning.[17]

Fight the fault lines. Every class, no matter how cohesive, probably has subgroups within it. There are best-friend pairs, small cliques, and transient alliances based on academics, sports, and social interests. There are also hard divisions based on race, ethnic background, and socioeconomic status. The fault lines that separate students from one another can fragment a class and create an environment that is stressful for all students, even those with the highest status and the most power. Such an environment works against learning.

While you are never going to eliminate jealousies and rivalries, you can limit them. As noted earlier, it helps to make it clear that bullying, name calling, and rudeness are not acceptable behavior in your class. When they occur, make it clear to the one committing the offense that he has disappointed you. It also helps to rearrange the seating chart from time to time. Students often dislike being moved around, but it helps them get to know students who might otherwise be in their "out" group.

Cooperative group work with random assignment to groups is another way to minimize the fault lines.[18] Social psychologist Elliot Aronson developed a form of group work explicitly designed to reduce tensions among students. He calls it jigsaw teaching.[19] The teacher assigns students to groups. Each person within the group learns about one part of a subject, and then shares what she has learned with the rest of the group. Students are held accountable for all aspects of the topic, not just the one they researched. This means that each student is dependent on every other student in the group. Students who ridicule or ostracize a member of their group are working against themselves, so cooperativeness tends to win the day. Of course, students could be pleasant and cooperative in the group, and then resume their hostile stance later. But as the students get to know one another in the groups, it becomes harder to snub them elsewhere. The result is improved morale and a better climate for learning.

Finally, you can discourage fault lines by not contributing to them yourself. Unfortunately, teachers often do just that. Teachers discriminate on the basis of gender, learning ability, race or ethnic group, physical attractiveness, and even seat location (students in the front seats versus those in the back).[20]

Encourage enthusiasm. Most people agree that it is a good thing for students to be enthusiastic about learning. Unfortunately, most of those same people forget that to be enthusiastic is to be emotional. It is a great mistake to think that students can be simultaneously enthusiastic and utterly quiet, still, and docile.

In an article called *Why Football Is Better than High School*, Herb Childress compares life in the classroom with life on the football field. Much of the difference has to do with emotion. "In football," he writes, "emotions and human contact are expected parts of the work. When players do well, they get to be happy. When they do poorly, they get to be angry."[21] If we want students to be enthusiastic about academic achievement, we have to allow them—no, we have to *encourage* them—to feel good about their successes and bad about their failures.

One way for teachers to encourage enthusiasm in students is to show some enthusiasm themselves. In a survey of teenagers, 71% of those polled said that the enthusiasm of teachers for their subjects was an important influence on what students learned, but only 29% of these students said that their teachers were enthusiastic.[22] I suspect that these teens underestimated their teachers, but this is one of those situations in which perception is reality: If teachers do not openly display enthusiasm for their subjects and for the achievements of their students, then they are not enthusiastic.

I cannot help but think that historian James Banner and classicist Harold Cannon were right when they asked,

> When a class masters a difficult subject, should not a teacher's spirits soar? And should not pride, admiration, and praise be among students' rewards for learning? If students and their teachers fail to experience feelings of joy, happiness, even occasional giddiness as they learn and develop together, then something is wrong.[23]

If teachers don't show that they care when students do well and are disappointed when they do poorly, then they should not be surprised if their students don't care, either. When renowned behaviorist B. F. Skinner invented the teaching machine, some teachers worried that the machines would put them out of work. Skinner replied, "Any teacher who *can* be replaced by a machine, *should* be."[24] He was not suggesting that teaching machines (now in the form of computers) are better than teachers. On the contrary, he was suggesting that any teacher worthy of the name offers things that *no machine can*. One of those things is an emotional connection with the student. Skinner knew that no student ever solved a math problem, wrote an essay, or painted a picture and then ran to show her work to a machine.

How often do we see a student giving a classmate a "high five" when he answers a difficult question correctly? How often are students permitted to cheer their teammates' successes in a spelling bee? No one objects to this kind of behavior at a Pee Wee soccer practice or on the basketball court, but it is virtually taboo in the classroom. Where is it written that academic work should be done without laughter, anger, or tears?

On discovering that an object displaces water in proportion to its density, Archimedes is said to have jumped from his bath and run naked in the street, shouting, "Eureka!" The story may be apocryphal, but it accurately portrays the excitement that scientists and scholars feel when they solve a difficult problem. Why shouldn't students be permitted to get a little excited when they solve a difficult problem? And if learning really does matter, how can we expect students to act with indifference when their efforts are unsuccessful?

Yes, things can get out of hand. Student emotions, once stirred, can threaten to turn an orderly class into a maelstrom. But there are not very many riots during football practice. If coaches are able to keep a lid on the emotions of students on an athletic field, teachers should be able to do so with students in a classroom.

Know your kids. Teaching is built on a foundation of knowledge—and that includes a teacher's knowledge of her students. When you first meet someone, what is the first thing you tell him about yourself? Our identity begins with our name. The teacher's first challenge with a new group of students is therefore to learn each and every student's name.

Experienced teachers use several tricks to help them do this. One is to use a seating chart. Having students sit in the same chair each day accomplishes two things: First, by consulting the seating chart you can figure out who a given student is and call on him by name instead of saying, "Yes, the boy in the back with the green Mohawk, you have a question?" Second, a seating chart helps you learn the names because you can try to recall each student's name and check your recall by referring to the chart. Otherwise you have no way of practicing except to ask the student, "Is your name Chanticleer?" Once you've learned the students' names, you can allow them to sit anywhere they like, although many teachers prefer to keep the assigned seats to prevent students from gathering into troublesome clusters.

Another common practice is to use imagery and word association. A redheaded student whose name is Eric obviously becomes Eric the Red. A girl with blond hair named Mary might become Mary (Lynn) Monroe. If Mary is a high school student who always wears a ring, you might think of it as a wedding ring; then you'll remember that she is "Mary'd."

Teachers do not ordinarily share these mnemonics with students, of course. Sometimes they are not very flattering, and if students were to learn of them they might become aggravating nicknames that the victims would have to endure for years to come. The purpose of the mnemonic is not to characterize the student, but to provide a clue that may stir your gray matter into producing the student's name.

If you teach five different groups of students, you may have 150 or more students. Learning that many names can be a challenge—especially when you have reached the age at which you can no longer remember at lunch what you ate for breakfast. Some years ago I had an inspiration that was a big help: On the first day of class I took a disposable camera.[25] I had students cluster together in groups of two or three, and I took their photographs. Later, I cut up the photos and pasted each student's image on one side of a 3 × 5 card with the student's name on the back of the card. Then I had a set of flash cards for each class, and I could learn the name that went with each face, the same way I would learn the synonyms for a set of Spanish nouns.

I always explain to students beforehand why I am taking the photographs. The announcement never fails to astonish the students, and it is a great icebreaker. They laugh as they mug for the camera and make jokes. After taking the first photograph, I turn the camera over to a student in that first cluster and ask him or her to get a few students together and take their photograph, then pass the camera along to another student, and so on.

This works extremely well with college students, and I would not hesitate to do it with middle or high school students. With a younger group, there is the risk of establishing a boisterous, party-like atmosphere, and of getting a collection of photographs of thumbs and blurred heads, so I would be inclined to take the pictures myself.

About midway through the first class I abruptly announce, "Well, time for a quiz." This provides another surprise for the students, who are then greatly relieved and even more astonished when I explain that it is I, and not they, who will be taking the quiz. "Let's see how many of your names I can recall," I say.

I then take the students in turn, offering a name. At the end of the class, I give myself the same quiz again. Naturally, I do not want to perform poorly on these quizzes, so my motivation for learning is good. Students are always impressed, and usually amazed, that an instructor would (a) take learning their names so seriously and (b) risk the humiliation of looking stupid in front of the class. I believe this helps to establish that our classroom is a place where it is safe to risk making mistakes.

There is, of course, no reason why you can't use all of these devices—seating chart, mnemonics, photo flash cards, and teacher quizzes. The point is to do whatever you can to learn the students' names in the shortest possible time.

Getting to know students means more than learning their names, of course. It means learning something about them as individuals. Many teachers ask students to complete a survey with questions about hobbies, special talents or interests, favorite books or movies, and (with all but the youngest students) life goals. Other teachers ask the students to write a brief autobiography.

Some teachers spend part of the first class by having students introduce themselves. This practice is not always successful. Adolescents in particular are often reluctant to talk about themselves before a group, and many of them seem to be so preoccupied with thinking about what they will say that they don't hear the other introductions. Since one of the goals of these introductions is for the students to get to know one another, this is counterproductive.

I have more success when I ask students to pair off with a neighbor and interview each other, and then to take turns introducing the person they interviewed. Many students find it less stressful to talk about a classmate than about themselves, perhaps because it is like the gossiping that they enjoy so much.

These information-gathering techniques suggest that the teacher is interested in students individually, but if the teacher does nothing with the information the exercises are largely wasted. Study the material you obtain and remember at least one significant thing about as many students as possible, then make reference to this information. For example, you might say, during a discussion of Poe's *The Raven*, "Sarah, I seem to remember that you enjoy bird watching. Does the raven in Poe's poem seem believable to you? Could a real raven act that way?"

Students know that you can't remember a lot of facts about every student. But if you remember a few facts about some of your students, that tells them all that you are interested in them as individuals, and that is important in establishing a learning climate.

Read the signs. Social psychologist Robert Rosenthal and his students have made a special study of the ways in which people communicate feelings through facial expression, tone of voice, and body language.[26] They have found that people vary a good deal in their skill at reading these nonverbal cues, and teachers tend to be pretty good at it. They need to be.[27] Students convey a good deal of information nonverbally about the effectiveness of a lesson, and teachers who can read these cues have access to an early warning system that can help them avoid stormy weather.

The signs of a deteriorating environment include drooping eyelids, slumped shoulders, yawns, window staring, sluggish replies, irritability, squirming, clock watching, and lackluster participation. The repair may be as simple as turning the thermostat down a notch or opening a window. Often a humorous remark puts a spark into a gloomy group. Laughing oxygenates the blood and increases blood flow to the brain, and this helps arouse students who are sinking toward dreamland.[28] Occasional humor also relieves tension and makes students more willing to tackle difficult tasks—such as decimals.[29]

Now and then, a short break from serious work also can do wonders for flagging spirits. Simply having students stand beside their desks and do a bit of Tai Chi, play Simon Says (perhaps modified to provide practice in some learned skill), or perform some stretching exercises can help. A game, a puzzle, or a contest offers diversion and an entirely new reason to take an interest in learning. The student who doesn't care a bean about the spelling of *parallel* may take delight in learning it, if it will help him defeat those smug girls in a boys-versus-girls spelling bee.

If the students are too excited, a shift in topic to something serious, even somber, may dampen the fires (a reading of Robert Frost's *Stopping by Woods on a Snowy Evening*, for example). Younger students may throttle down if directed to put their heads on their desks for a brief rest, and if the teacher closes the blinds and yawns a few times beforehand the students may "catch" his sleepiness and welcome a nap.

Signs that there is a chronic problem with the climate include students who are frequently uncooperative, irritable, tardy, or absent. Your own feelings are also a clue. If you are not enjoying your time with the students, chances are that something is amiss and you are headed for trouble. If you can't figure out where the problem lies, have a chat in a quiet moment with some of the students; they may point out problems you didn't know existed.[30]

A lot goes into establishing and maintaining a good learning climate, but the effort is worth it. Students learn more and are better behaved and everyone, including the teacher, goes home feeling better about their day.

If you are able to establish a good climate for learning, then you and your students can go almost anywhere. To get there, though, you need to . . .

2

Define the Destination

> *You've got to be very careful if you don't know where you're going, because you might not get there.*
>
> —Yogi Berra

As part of their training, all teachers should take up orienteering. That's the sport in which people strive to find their way from point A to point B, often slogging through swamps, fighting vicious briars, and dodging poison ivy, with nothing more than a map and a compass to guide them. The object is to be the first person to arrive at the appointed destination. Orienteering is a good way to develop skill at map reading, compass use, and problem solving. It might also help teachers appreciate the value of having a clear idea of where they want to take their students.

Of course, every teacher has some general idea of what he wants to accomplish—to inspire students, to get them excited about learning, to help them grow as human beings, to civilize them, to help them become productive citizens, and so on.

Such lofty goals are certainly admirable and appropriate, but teaching isn't a matter of giant leaps. In orienteering, you don't get from A to B in a single bound, but rather by small steps that take you to intermediate points along the way. To do that, you always need to know where you are and where you're going. In the same way, the teacher moves by taking small steps to a series of intermediate points, and she must always know where she is and where she is going.

Hence, this brief discussion of a subject most educators consider tedious, many consider passé, and some consider hateful—the writing of instructional objectives. Old fashioned and unpopular it may be, but putting objectives into words is a critical part of teaching, since it defines what is to be taught. To be most effective, instructional objectives should have four characteristics.

First, a good instructional objective specifies what the student will be able to do if a lesson is successful. Most goal statements pretend to do this, but in fact they do not. Look in a curriculum guide and you are likely to find a gazillion objectives, but in many guides few tell you what the student should be able to do. Typical goal statements in curriculum guides include:

- The student will *know* the alphabet (or numbers, the colors of the spectrum, the Chinese kanji for 100 words, etc.)
- The student will *understand* the law of gravity (or photosynthesis, the process of law making, the concept of perspective, etc.).
- The student will *appreciate* the short story (or abstract art, contemporary poetry, classical music, etc.).

You may be thinking, "What's so bad about these statements? A kid should know the alphabet; what's wrong with that?" The problem is that the statements are vague. There is no way for the teacher, or anyone else, to say whether the goal has been achieved.[1] Expressions such as *know, understand,* and *appreciate* often show up in educational goal statements because they seem to convey what is to be accomplished. But what exactly does it mean to know, understand, and appreciate? When we ask that question, we begin to see how little value these words have for setting goals.

You may want students to "know their numbers" from 1 to 10, for example, but what does that mean, exactly? Does it mean that, when asked to count to ten, the student recites, "1, 2, 3," and so on to 10? That he can count downward from 10 to 1? That she knows that 7 is a bigger number than 6? That, given a display of eight items on a table and asked to count them, he can tell you how many there are? That she can tell you that a table with 9 items has more items than a table with 8 items? Ultimately, "knowing your numbers" means all of these things and more, but the teacher cannot teach all of these things in one lesson. Each time she teaches students the numbering system, she must decide what exactly she wants them to be able to *do* at the end of the lesson.

Similarly, what does it mean to *understand* the law of gravity? Does it mean that, given four equations and asked to identify the one that represents the law of gravity, the student picks the right one? Does it mean that he can write the mathematical law of gravity when asked to? That he can express it in his own words? That he can use the law to solve problems, such as determining whether a hypothetical comet would collide with earth?

Appreciation is even more troublesome as a goal. Everyone wants students to develop an appreciation of art, music, and literature, but how do we know when the student appreciates them? Is a student who appreciates art one who shows evident pleasure in looking at paintings? One who paints in his or her spare time? One who argues with other students about the relative merits of Maxfield Parish and M. C. Escher? Inadequate as these definitions may be, we can define appreciation of art (or music, literature, or scientific method) only in terms of what an appreciative student will *do*.

I am not arguing that *knowing* the alphabet, *understanding* gravity and *appreciating* the short story and the like are worthless goals. I am arguing that unless you can translate these and similar terms into student behavior, you have not really identified your goals and can have little hope of achieving them.[2] By way of example, here are some instructional objectives stated in a way that can guide the teacher as he or she works:

- The student will count from 1 to 10 without error or hesitation.

- The student will recite the formal expression of the law of gravity and paraphrase it in his or her own words.

• The student will willingly read short stories of his or her choosing with evident pleasure when given the opportunity.

None of these objectives statements is perfect. What does it mean, for example, to say that a student can count from 1 to 10 without hesitation? If he recites the numbers steadily at the rate of one every two seconds, is that without hesitation? What if he pauses less than one second between most of the numbers but takes four seconds between 5 and 6? Many objectives can be defined to get around such problems, and doing so is often worthwhile. We could say, for example, "The student will recite the numbers from 1 to 10 without error in 10 seconds." The important thing, however, is that the teacher's attention is focused on what the student actually does, not on something that may or may not be lodged between his ears. If a student counts at the rate of one number per second, one teacher may consider that performance fluent and another may not; but both are paying attention to the student's performance.

It is often said that teaching changes the student, but if there is a change, it is that the student can do something that he or she could not do before. A good instructional objective specifies what that something is. As Neil Postman and Charles Weingartner suggested long ago, "if you do not act as if you know something, then you do not know it."[3]

Second, a good instructional objective provides an achievable challenge. This sounds easy, but it is a delicate matter. If the teacher underestimates what the students can accomplish, he risks boring them and holding them back. If he is overly optimistic about his students, he runs the risk of creating confusion and frustration. The ideal is to set the fruit so that it is well within reach—if the student stands on tiptoe.

Since no one can predict with certainty what a given student or group of students will accomplish on a given day, the teacher must keep her finger on the student pulse and be prepared to modify her goals as necessary.

Third, a good instructional objective is shared with the student. It is not just the teacher who needs to know what the destination is; students also need to know where they are headed. A brief statement helps students follow the lesson: "Today, you're going to begin to learn your ABCs"; "Now I'm going to teach you how to tell complete sentences from incomplete sentences, called fragments"; "You know what an equation is. Today you're going to learn how to use an equation to solve a problem." As Daniel Seymour and Terry Seymour write, "By drawing students' attention to our objectives at the beginning of a lesson, throughout the lesson, and at the end, we help them focus on key things to learn."[4]

Fourth, a good instructional objective is written. It is tempting to tell oneself, "I know what I want to accomplish in this lesson; I don't need to write it down." But what often happens is that when you attempt to write

"We're going to be exploring new frontiers, right Mr. Whipple?"

George B. Abbott

what you want to accomplish, you find that you're not as sure of your goals as you thought. You needn't write an essay; a short sentence will do, so long as you specify what the student will need to do to convince you that you have achieved your goal.

By now, you may be thinking that the idea of writing brief instructional objectives is a no-brainer. "Why," you may be wondering, "would anyone *not* do this?" But in fact some educators are vehemently opposed to writing instructional objectives, especially those that focus on behavior.[5] The critics typically offer three reasons for their opposition:

1. *Critics say that written objectives make the instructional process rigid.* Writing objectives, they claim, squelches spontaneity, constrains creativity, and prevents the teacher from making use of "the teachable moment."

2. *Critics say that writing objectives results in undue emphasis on facts and low-level skills.* The idea is that objectives having to do with facts and simple skills are easier to write than those that have to do with more advanced kinds of knowledge and skill, such as critical thinking and originality, which therefore are neglected.

3. *Critics say that many of the things we want students to learn cannot be expressed in terms of actions.* Learning produces mysterious changes deep within the student, but these changes may never reveal themselves in the student's behavior.

I find these arguments against objectives unconvincing, and I offer the following rebuttal:

First, regarding the idea that written objectives put teachers into straightjackets: It is true that written objectives help to focus and structure the lesson, but that is a good thing. It contributes to an orderly classroom, and good order is conducive to learning. That is not merely my opinion and the opinion of many experienced teachers, it is also the opinion of a majority of students, including those who are not models of studiousness. Students need and want structure and focus.

Second, regarding the emphasis on low-level skills: If there is a tendency for teachers to write objectives that emphasize facts and lower-level skills, then that is surely a reflection of what teachers do *without* written objectives.[6] It is absurd to suggest that a teacher would be teaching higher-level skills if only she did not write objectives. On the contrary, if a teacher has a bias toward lower-level skills, writing objectives may at least make this bias apparent to her. The result may be an epiphany and a change of direction: "Hey, most of my objectives deal with facts. Maybe I should think about some higher-level kinds of things."

Third, regarding the idea that important learning does not reveal itself in behavior: We are asked to take this on faith. Any demonstration would involve student behavior, which would contradict the thesis. But let's leave that to the philosophers. For us it is enough that many things students need to learn *can* be revealed in behavior, and it is certainly desirable to identify these achievements as goals.

Yes, there are times when circumstances will lead a teacher to drop one planned objective in favor of another. Sometimes, for example, the most important goal is to restore good will in a student whose feelings have just been crushed by another student's remark. But the teacher who sees his day as a series of specific challenges, with each challenge spelled out clearly as a performance objective, will get better results than the teacher, however well-intentioned, who hasn't a clue what he wants his students to be able to do at the end of the day.

Once a teacher has a clear idea where she wants to take her students, she is ready to . . .

3

Show the Way

> *Show me.*
>   —Missouri state motto

I stand in front of a group of college students. Without saying a word, I hand each student a blank sheet of paper. Then, still without a word, I hold up a sheet of paper just like theirs. As the students look on, I fold the paper in two, then look at the class and wait. Soon they imitate my action.[1]

I make another fold as the students watch, then I wait for them to follow my lead. This continues until my paper forms a hinged pair of pyramids, each with its own "pocket." I put my thumb in one pocket, and two fingers in the other, and wait for the students to follow suit. Then I operate the puppet I have created—the two pyramids opening and closing like a mouth. I announce, "You have now created your very own cootie catcher," and I quickly reach for the head of the nearest student as if to remove a cootie (that ill-defined but ever feared playground pest) from his hair.

This lesson takes about five minutes, a lot of time to devote to creating a silly toy, but it makes a powerful point—you can teach people a lot without saying a word, just by showing them what to do.

The word *teach* comes from a word that means to lead or show the way. The most elementary form of showing the way is to demonstrate or model what is to be done. We literally do this when we signal others to follow us and then lead where we want them to go.

Modeling is the most ancient way of teaching, one that undoubtedly preceded the development of language. A boy learned to make a bow mainly by watching as an experienced adult made one. Rituals, dances, the making of tools and weapons—all were learned mainly by watching experienced adults. The same sort of modeling forms the basis of much of the educational effort of people in industrialized nations today.

Modeling is especially likely to be used when the task involves a series of steps, such as in tying a shoelace or operating a computer. Ask any man who has taught his son how to tie a necktie, and I doubt if you'll find any who did it solely with words. As Lewis Carroll's Dodo reminds us, "The best way to explain it is to do it."

Pictures, models, diagrams, graphs, and tables also can be used to *show* the student a point, often better than that point can be expressed in words. Indeed, adding words to a good demonstration sometimes contributes nothing. Ian Tattersall describes a study in which college students learned to make a primitive tool.[2] Some students received both verbal instructions and a demonstration, while others saw only the demonstration. Learning proceeded just as well in both groups.

Yet words can often help. You might teach your kids how to tell time by making a cardboard clock face with hands you can move, but wordlessly moving the hands to different positions will not suffice; you must *tell* them what the positions mean. It might go something like this:

TEACHER: "When the big hand is on the 12 and the little hand is on the 9, it is 9 o'clock. (You arrange the hands accordingly as you explain.)

STUDENT: "That's when the school bell rings."

TEACHER: "Yes, that's right. And when the big hand and the small hand are both on the 12 . . . (you arrange the hands) it is 12 o'clock."

STUDENT: "When we go to lunch!"

TEACHER: "That's right."

Similarly, if you are teaching students about negative numbers, you might draw a thermometer on the board and ask the students to read several temperatures, starting with 100 and working your way down to zero:

"It's getting colder and colder. Now it's down to 5 degrees. It gets colder and the mercury drops to here (you point to two degrees). How cold is it now, Juan?"

"Two degrees."

"Right. Now it gets colder (you point to zero degrees). Now what's the temperature, Samantha?"

"Zero."

"Right. But it's getting even colder, colder than zero degrees. The mercury is down here (you point to an undefined point below zero). What is the temperature now, George?

"Uhm, uh, zero."

"No it was zero up here (you point to zero degrees), but it's *colder* than that now. We need to show that it's colder than zero. How could we do that?"

"Add some numbers below the zero?"

"Good idea. (You write 1, 2, 3, 4, 5 in the space below zero.) Now the mercury is here (you point to 5 below zero), so what is the temperature now, Jamal?"

"Five degrees."

"Five degrees. Right. Oh, wait a minute! There's a problem, isn't there? Does anyone see the problem?"

"You have two five degrees, and one is colder than the other."

"That's it exactly, Howie. I'll tell you what: All these numbers (you point above the zero) are *more* than zero, so let's put a plus beside them (you write plusses next to some numbers), and all of these number are *less* than zero, so let's put a minus sign next to them (you make minus signs). Now, what can we call this temperature (you point to 5 below), Hisae?"

"Maybe you could call it minus 5?"

"Excellent idea."

Much of a teacher's talk should be an attempt to model in words what cannot be modeled in other ways. But there are other good reasons for teachers to talk. Words can simplify the complex, clarify the confusing, highlight key features, note differences, and elaborate on a theme. Consider the student who is confused by adjectives and adverbs. He asks:

"Adjectives and adverbs . . . I don't know, they seem the same to me."

"Well, do you remember the definition of an adjective?"

"It's a word that modifies a noun."

"Right. It tells us something about a person, place or thing. And what does an adverb do?"

"It tells us about a verb. Like, 'The horse ran quickly.' *Quickly* tells us how he ran. But, I don't know, aren't they really the same?"

"Ah, yes. You're right! Both modify another part of speech. The difference is that one modifies nouns, the other modifies verbs and adverbs. If I changed your sentence to 'The black horse ran quickly,' what word would *black* modify?"

"Horse."

"Right. So in this sentence, *black* is . . . ?"

"An adjective? Because it modifies a noun."

"Exactly. Adjectives and adverbs are similar, but there is a difference. Does that help?"

"I guess so." (Don't be disappointed by "I guess so." You won't always get an emphatic "Yes!")

The teacher here is showing the student the distinction that he finds troubling, just as you might point to a divide in a road and say, "Both of these roads go to Modunk, but the one on the right goes through a valley and the one on the left goes over a mountain."

In some cases, showing the way relies very heavily on words. Teaching the parts of speech, the philosophy of Schopenhauer, or Freud's theory of personality structure solely through modeling and graphics would be very difficult, if not impossible. But we ought not to talk when it is more effective to show. You can talk forever about the characteristics of good writing, for example, without ever improving a student's writing.

Show your students something that is well written or, better yet, show them how to modify a poor composition in a way that makes it better, and your students can *see* what good writing looks like. Similarly, an art teacher can lecture about shading for hours without improving a student's skill as much as she would in a minute by making a few strokes with a piece of charcoal.

Words are also a way of modeling skills the instructor cannot demonstrate. Bela Karolyi, the women's gymnastic coach who helped the careers of Nadia Comaneci and Mary Lou Retton, among others, is a big, burly man. It is difficult to imagine him demonstrating a forward roll, much less the complicated moves required on the uneven parallel bars. His body simply isn't capable of modeling what his pixie gymnasts must do. He might have his students watch videos and films of gymnasts performing different skills, but when he realizes that a student needs to modify a movement, it is likely that he relies heavily on words to show the way.

When teaching complex skills, it is often quite possible and usually desirable to teach the thought processes involved. Usually the best way to do this is to model the skills by thinking aloud. For example, suppose you want to teach students how to calculate a 15% tip on a restaurant bill in their heads. You should begin by making sure the students can do the calculations on paper, that they know how to multiply by 10% (by moving the decimal in the multiplicand one place to the left), and that they can divide any two-digit number in half without paper and pencil. Then the lesson might go something like this:

> Let's suppose you're in a restaurant and you want to leave a 15% tip. You don't have pencil and paper or a calculator, so you have to do it in your head. Let's try it. The bill is $14 and you want to leave a 15% tip. See if you can tell me the answer—without using pencil and paper. . . .

More than likely, the students will attempt to solve the problem in their heads the same way they would on paper. (You will probably see some of them "scribbling" on their desk or in the air using their forefingers as pencils.) Most people find this task very difficult, so few if any students are likely to come up with the correct answer. You continue:

> If you try to do it in your head the same way you do it on paper, it's very difficult. Let me show you an easier way. Now, let's see. (You do the calculations on the board so the students can follow easily.) To get 10% of $14, I just move the decimal one place to the left; that gives me $1.40. So a 10% tip would be $1.40. I want to leave 15%; 15% is 10% plus 5%, so I need to add half of the 10% tip to the $1.40. Half of $1.40 is $.70, so I add that to $1.40. Seventy cents and $1.40 make $2.10. So the tip is $2.10.

If you see puzzled faces (and you probably will), you will need to go through the process again, preferably with the same or very similar problem. When the students seem to "get it," give them an *easier* problem, such as figuring a 15% tip on $10, and ask them to solve it in their heads. When they have the answer, ask a student to think aloud to demonstrate how he or she did it. Now provide a slightly harder problem, such as calculating a 15% tip on $20.

The thinking required for solving problems in writing, history, science, and so on can be modeled in this same way. We can say to students, "Think!" but such exhortations are of little benefit to students who don't know what that means. Thinking skills, like any others, have to be learned, and the best way to teach them is by modeling them—that is, by thinking aloud as you work on problems.

When you demonstrate a skill, you are teaching not only the steps for performing that skill but also more subtle aspects, such as persistence, thoughtfulness, flexibility, and tactics. In one study, children watched as a model worked on problems. Some models worked hard and eventually reached a solution; other models made a halfhearted attempt and failed. The children later worked on a problem themselves. Those who had watched a persistent model kept at their problem longer than children who had not seen a model. Those who had seen the model who quit gave up even sooner than children who had seen no model. So, be careful what you model!

When we think of teaching, we usually think of providing exemplary demonstrations or descriptions of a skill, concept or principle, but there are times when a less-than-exemplary model is useful. Students can learn *not* to make common mistakes if the mistakes and their adverse consequences are demonstrated. For example, in watercolor painting, you can easily ruin a fine painting by continuing to "perfect" it. A water color teacher might caution students, "Don't do too much," but the lesson will be better learned if the teacher illustrates it by taking a picture she has painted and making "improvements" that ultimately diminish its beauty. Similarly, a language instructor may pronounce foreign words both correctly and incorrectly to illustrate the difference between proper and improper pronunciation: "Notice that the Spanish word for *dog* is pronounced peRRRRRoo (rolling the r's), not pair-oooo. Listen to the difference: peRRRRRRRRRooo, *not* pair-ooo."

Sometimes it is very useful to make "accidental" errors, called foolers. The errors should be unambiguous, and they should be made at a point when the students have pretty well mastered the content and so are likely to catch the error. For example, suppose you have taught a lesson on multiplying two-digit numbers, such as 48 × 22. You've done a few problems with the students on the board and you are reviewing:

> "Let's do one more just to be sure everyone understands. OK, 48 times 22 (you write the problem on the board.) Two times 8 is 16, write down 6, two times 4 is 8, write down 8, now. . . (you hear some tittering) What? What are you laughing at—Mary?"
>
> "You made a mistake!"
>
> "A mistake? I did?"
>
> "You forgot to carry the 1. Two times 8 is 16, so you have to write 6 and carry 1. Then 2 times 4 is 8, you add 1 and that makes 9. So you should have written *96*, not 86!"
>
> "You're right! I'm glad you caught that. So this is 96 (you change 86 to 96). Now, 2 times 8 is 16, write 6, *carry 1* (you look at Mary and give her a wink), 2 times 4 is 8, plus 1 is *9*. . . ."

An occasional fooler can be very useful. It helps keep the students alert—they have to be alert to play the game of "catch the teacher"—and it helps you determine how confident the students are about what they've learned. And if you take correction from the students well, you show that mistakes are not tragedies. If mistakes do not embarrass the teacher ("Oh, you're right, Bill. I forgot to carry the 1. Thank you for pointing that out."), then the students need not be embarrassed at the mistakes *they* make. Of course, if the students *don't* catch a mistake, you may have to give some hints.

Some teachers don't like the idea of making mistakes deliberately. It's true that it can be overdone. You are essentially demonstrating what *not* to do, and too much of that can be confusing. But if you are fairly confident that your kids have "got it," a fooler adds a bit of fun to the lesson. If the students don't notice a mistake, you can always announce that there's a problem with your solution and challenge the students to find it.

You might worry that foolers will make students think the teacher is stupid, but a *competent* teacher doesn't need to worry about that since his true mistakes will be infrequent. In that case, the students will soon realize that the foolers are a kind of game you play, so they will not hold the errors against you.

Some educators today actually encourage students to make mistakes ("Good! You made a mistake. That means you're learning."), but in my view that goes too far. I do not want to encourage students to do slipshod work on the grounds that "mistakes are good." And if students are encouraged to make mistakes, learning is undermined by the *stubborn error effect*: the tendency we have to remember errors but to forget that they are errors.[3]

The stubborn error effect is exacerbated by the common practice of inducing the student to turn one mistake into several mistakes. Consider the case of the student who does not know how to spell the word spinach:

TEACHER: Spell spinach, Alfred.

ALFREDO: Spinach . . . s-p-i-n-i-t-c-h.

TEACHER: No, that's not right. Think about it, and try again.

ALFREDO: Uhm . . . s-p-e-n-a-g-e.

TEACHER: No, no, no. Try one more time.

ALFREDO: S-p-i-n-e-d-g-e.

Even if Alfred gets lucky and spells the word correctly, he will have made more wrong attempts than correct ones, so he's more likely to spell spinach incorrectly in the future as a result of this "instructional" exercise.

Instead of encouraging the student to make additional errors, it makes more sense to correct the student's error immediately and then have him perform the task correctly:

TEACHER: Spell spinach, Alfred.

ALFREDO: Spinach . . . s-p-i-n-i-t-c-h.

TEACHER: No, that's not right. Listen: s-p-i-n-*A*-c-h. Now you try it.

ALFREDO: s-p-i-n-*A*-c-h.

TEACHER: That's right. Try it again.

ALFREDO: s-p-i-n-*A*-c-h.

TEACHER: Right. And again. . . .

ALFREDO (in quick succession): s-p-i-n-a-c-h.

Once a mistake is made, teachers can reduce the likelihood of its repetition by requiring the student to correct the mistake immediately and repeatedly. For example, if a student writes "recieve," it may not be enough to point out the error and remind her of the rule, "Use i before e except after c. . . ." You might need to have her write "receive" several times. The best defense against the stubborn error effect, however, is to limit the number of mistakes. Teachers can do this by proceeding in small steps, monitoring student progress, and by providing hints when necessary to prompt correct answers.

In addition to foolers, it is useful to provide examples and non-examples.[4] To know what a car is, for example, is to be able to discriminate accurately between cars and other vehicles. It is helpful to give a rule that defines the concept, but that in itself is unlikely to be sufficient; you also need to provide examples and non-examples. For instance, you may say, "A car is a motorized vehicle used mostly to transport a few passengers. (You hold up two pictures side by side.) This (you raise the photograph of a 1954 Ford Thunderbird) is a car. This (you lower the Thunderbird picture and raise a picture of a garbage truck) is not."

After you've shown several examples and non-examples, you can begin challenging the students to identify cars. You can do this by presenting examples and non-examples side by side and asking, "Which one is a car?" or you can present one item at a time in random order and ask, "Is this a car?"

In the early stages of learning it is best to make the examples and non-examples very different, as in my example of the T-bird and the garbage truck. When the students begin to answer correctly, gradually make the examples more and more similar, each time pointing out (or having students point out) the key differences that allow you to say that one item is a car and the other is something else:

"What do you think about this one, Charles? Is it a car?"

"No."

"That's right. This is a train. It's not a car because it runs on tracks."

Your examples and non-examples should get progressively closer until the distinction is subtle. Be careful to monitor your students' performance. If you find they are having trouble making fine distinctions, end the session and continue it another day. It helps to let students "live with" new ideas for a time.

It is sometimes useful to teach two concepts at the same time. For example, in teaching geometric shapes, you might teach squares and rectangles simultaneously. You give the definition of a square and show a square, then give the definition of a rectangle and show a rectangle. You then present a series of paired figures (one rectangle and one square) side by side, and ask the students to identify each, or you present the figures alone, alternating randomly between rectangles and squares.

Be sure to start with simple line drawings that are exactly the same in size, color, and other features. The only difference should be that one forms a square and the other forms a rectangle. If you present them side-by-side, vary the location of the two kinds of figures. If the square is always on the teacher's left, the students will learn to call anything on the teacher's left a square. If you present the figures one at a time, be sure to randomize the sequence or the students will reason that, "the last one was a square, so this must be a rectangle." Next begin introducing irrelevant features. Hold up a red square and a blue rectangle, then compare a large rectangle with a small square, and so on.

Much more sophisticated concepts can also be taught using this same basic procedure. Medical students must, for example, learn to distinguish between diseases with similar symptoms:

> "Imagine that you are a physician in general practice. A forty-year-old female comes to see you. She has a productive cough, a high fever, poor pallor, malaise, and weakness. You also notice that there is blood on the handkerchief she uses to cover her mouth when she coughs. What is the more likely illness, flu or tuberculosis? Yes, Mr. Bradley?"
>
> "Tuberculosis?"
>
> "Right. Why did you say so?"
>
> "She has blood on her handkerchief, so she's probably coughing blood, which is a symptom of TB but not usually of flu."
>
> "Good."

The instructor might also present two hypothetical cases side by side and ask the students, "Which one has TB?"

Eventually, of course, you will want to present examples and non-examples without any hints. You might hold up a photo of a vehicle and say, "What is this?" A medical school professor may describe a patient with a set of subtle symptoms and ask, "Based on these symptoms, what disease do you suspect the patient has?" But this level of instruction should come later, after the student has mastered less difficult challenges.

In showing the way, it is usually best to begin simply. A teacher who wants to teach the anatomy of the heart could provide a detailed, anatomically correct model or photographs of a dissected heart. But such sophisticated aids are actually *less* likely to help beginning students than a simple, crude line drawing on the chalkboard showing the heart's four chambers and arrows indicating the direction of the flow of blood. When the students understand this much, the teacher might add lines to indicate the valves that keep blood from flowing backward between heartbeats. This doesn't require any great artistic skill on the part of the teacher. A sketch that looks nothing at all like a real heart can be very effective, even something like this:

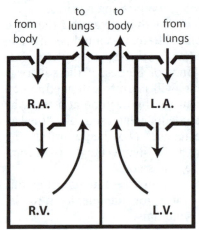

to   to
from   lungs body   from
body   lungs

R.A.   L.A.

R.V.   L.V.

Blood flows through the heart. This simple schematic shows that the heart is actually two pumps: one propels oxygen-depleted blood to the lungs; the other propels oxygen-rich blood to the body. R.A. indicates right atrium; R.V. is the right ventricle; L.A. is the left atrium; L.V. is the left ventricle. The gaps in the heart walls indicate valves.

The problem with realistic models, photographs, and sketches is that they can include too much information. Start with something simple, and gradually increase the complexity.

Some teachers will quarrel with this advice. "A surgeon doesn't open up a man's chest and operate on a box with four simple chambers in it," they insist. "Students need to learn to deal with reality." And so they do, but they don't have to *start* with reality. The teacher's job is to take the student as far as she can in the time she has. Usually the best way to do that is to begin simply, and gradually add complexity.

Gradually is the key word. I think there is a tendency for teachers to move too fast from simple tasks to complex ones. Sometimes the ideal way of teaching a skill is to demonstrate the solution of a problem on the board (or overhead projector or computer screen) and then, when students seem to understand, erase the solution and have the students work on *the very same problem* at their desks. This greatly reduces the difficulty and allows the student to go through the problem without agonizing over how to frame it. Of course, for some students working a problem that has just been solved by the teacher will be a waste of time, but many students will benefit from the exercise. In any case, it is important to increase the level of difficulty slowly enough that students are able to succeed.

Simplifying means limiting or eliminating unessential features and exaggerating key features. In teaching about different kinds of music, for example, you might play short selections from clear-cut examples of classical, jazz, rock, and so on. Later you can introduce selections that blend elements of different kinds of music.

When presenting information, you can go about it in one of two ways. The part-to-whole approach breaks the skill into logical components and then builds the components. The whole-to-part method provides an overview, the big picture, and then fills in the details.

In learning complex skills, it is usually better to go from part to whole. A gymnast who is going to perform a complex series of tumbling skills in the floor exercise would probably do well to learn each component of the routine thoroughly before attempting to put them together. Similarly, we teach students to write individual letters, then words, then sentences, then paragraphs, then essays, and *then* we teach them to write term papers.

There are times, however, when the whole-to-part approach is better. Learning to draw is one such task. In teaching students to draw a face, for example, you could begin with some feature of the face, such as the eye, and show the students how to draw that. When they can do this reasonably well, you might show them how to draw a nose, and have them attempt that, and so on. But this part-to-whole approach is probably not very useful in teaching portrait drawing, because the success of the complete figure depends a great deal on the relationships among the components. The eyes, nose, mouth, and so on must be properly oriented toward one another. Because of this, art teachers usually have students begin by drawing an ovoid shape for the head and then "roughing in" eyes, ears, nose, and chin. After this, the teacher shows how to make refinements on each of the features of the face. This whole-to-part approach works well in drawing not only human faces but also full-length portraits, animals, landscapes, buildings, bowls of fruit—anything.

In the same way, students sometimes write essays by constructing the first sentence and then rephrasing parts of it, checking spelling, checking punctuation, and so on. Then they write a second sentence and perfect that. Professional writers rarely work this way. Instead they focus at first on getting the overall story laid out in outline, then quickly write a rough draft, then correct major flaws, and lastly check for minor problems such as spelling errors. The teacher can demonstrate this process by, for example, jotting notes on the chalkboard about the things he wants to say in a composition and then arranging them in a logical order. This outline then guides his writing of the essay. He could next write a topic sentence for each paragraph represented in the outline, and then fill in supporting sentences. Or he might write a rough draft of each paragraph in turn. Finally, he will check each sentence for errors in spelling, capitalization, punctuation, and grammar.

The whole-to-part approach emphasizes important ideas over details and has the advantage of giving students an idea of where they are headed. The part-to-whole approach emphasizes small steps and has the advantage of simplifying the task and helping students master the skills they need to learn the next step.

Regardless of how you present information, the question of the pace of presentation arises. How quickly should you present information? Some authorities recommend a fast pace. It's stimulating and therefore discourages boredom. It animates students, who have to stay alert to keep up. And it covers a lot of ground. Research shows that, in general, the more information to which students are exposed, the more they learn.[5]

Those who favor a slower pace point out that when the pace is fast, some students may get left behind and become discouraged. This is especially true when the content requires mastering a series of steps, as in mathematics and science. A fast pace also discourages thoughtful comments and questions, since they inevitably take time. There is also reason to believe that comprehension declines as the rate of speech goes above 150 words per minute.[6]

Probably the best approach is to vary the pace, depending on the nature of the students' level of mastery and the difficulty of the material. If you are teaching new material, you might need to go slowly; if you are elaborating on material the students have studied earlier, you can try picking up the pace. If you are reviewing material the students have already mastered, the pace can be very quick indeed. Above all, you will need to set the pace based on the behavior of the students. You must monitor them closely, always scanning for the wrinkled brows and drooping eyelids that precede blank stares and snoring. When warning signs appear, it is time to change the pressure on the instructional accelerator.

The teacher is responsible for showing the way, but she doesn't have to do all the pointing herself. Students can and should learn from one another. The "show and tell" lesson in elementary grades is not merely a way of giving students practice in speaking before a group. It is also a way of teaching other students interesting things. Oral reports, debates, class discussions, and dramatizations are examples of things students can do that benefit their classmates as well as themselves. Indeed, I believe we miss much of the value of these exercises by neglecting their substance.

Peer tutoring is another way that students can learn from one another. In peer tutoring, the tutor sometimes learns as much as or more than the tutored.[7] Learning researcher B. R. Bugelski writes that there is no mystery in this:

> What is important is that the teacher-to-be begins to put in the necessary time to organize, to program, to check the facts, to tie the loose ends. The new teacher learns more than the new student because he works harder and longer at the job. The trick of teaching is to make all students teachers.[8]

Charles Greenwood and Joseph Delquadri developed a competitive system for class-wide peer tutoring.[9] Students form two teams, and the members of each team pair off. One student in each pair is a tutor, and the pairs earn points for their team as the tutored students progress. The students learn and have fun doing so.

Students occasionally object to being tutored by their peers. Sometimes this can be dealt with by having students take turns in the tutoring role. Sometimes the sessions can be construed as pair learning—that is, the students work together on a task and help each other learn. And of course, cross-age tutoring, in which older students tutor younger ones, is well accepted by the tutored students.[10]

Group work is another way of providing information, especially when each student learns about one aspect of a topic and then shares that information with other members of the group, as in the jigsaw method.[11]

Debates and mock trials are also useful. Each side of an issue (e.g., the legality of community curfews; whether immigrants should be allowed to become president; who actually wrote the works of Shakespeare) is represented by one or more students who present their case, including expert testimony by other class members, before a panel of three or more student judges.

Showing the way—through demonstration, visual aids, words, or student presentations—is at the very core of teaching. Yet there are other kinds of "delivery systems," as they are called in educationese, including the lecture, the Socratic (or inquiry) method, and discovery teaching. Each has some merit.

Lecture, as defined here, is continuous speech lasting more than five minutes that is only occasionally interrupted by students, usually to ask a question about a point just covered. The lecture is today a much maligned methodology, and deservedly so, for the most part. The consensus is that lectures are boring and ineffective.

Except, of course, when they are not. Some people can lecture in ways that excite students and result in a great deal of learning. Unfortunately, lecturers of this caliber are rare. If you ran for class office in high school and the students and faculty rose to their feet and cheered at your speeches, you might be a great lecturer, but otherwise don't count on it. You are more likely as boring a speaker as the rest of us. (Remember that one definition of a lecturer is a person who talks in someone else's sleep.)

However, the lecture has endured since the days of the ancient Greek coliseums for a reason: Even a boring speaker can reach a lot of people. With the aid of a good speaker system, a lecture can be delivered to an audience of 100 students—or 100,000. So, if you are called upon to teach 50,000 people in a football stadium, you might want to consider the lecture. But if your teaching is limited to a class of 30 or so students, some other method might be better.

Some teachers argue that boring lectures are part of life, especially college life, and that the teacher has a duty to prepare students for this hardship by exposing them to boring lectures. (Don't laugh. I've heard people make that case!) It's true that students can learn to endure lectures. They can be given very short lectures starting in, say, third grade, and these can be gradually stretched until, by grade 12, the student is exposed to lectures of 40 minutes or more. This no doubt will make college lectures of 50 minutes readily tolerated. But if you want students to learn as much as possible, you probably should keep lectures short and infrequent.[12] As psychologist Richard Malott of Western Michigan University likes to say, "Preachin' ain't teachin'."

The *Socratic method* is a better alternative. This approach gets its name from Socrates, the sage of ancient Greece, who taught by asking questions. To Socrates, knowledge resided in the individual and had only to be drawn out by the teacher. "We do not learn," Plato has Socrates say, "and what we call learning is only a process of recollection."

Socrates may well have been a brilliant teacher, but I think few people today accept his view of learning as remembering. (Are we really to believe that babies are born knowing that Hemingway was a writer, that the square of 12 is 144, and that Klingon is a fictitious alien language?) Instead, the Socratic teacher asks the student to use what he or she *does* know to make logical inferences, the inferences being new knowledge. Today the practice is often called *inquiry teaching*, meaning teaching by asking questions.[13] While inquiry teaching is a rather cumbersome way of teaching most subjects, it is probably an effective way of developing analytical thinking skills. Consider this exchange:

TEACHER: Can you give me an example of a mammal?

PHIL: I can't think of any just now.

TEACHER: Well, think about the animals you see every day. What animals have you seen today?

PHIL: I saw a dog on the way to school.

TEACHER: Is a dog a mammal?

PHIL: I think so.

TEACHER: You're right, it is. Can you tell me why?

PHIL: Hmmmm. . . . Not really.

TEACHER: Before you told me the definition of mammals. The definition included some characteristics of mammals. What was one of those characteristics?

PHIL: They usually have a lot of hair.

TEACHER: Does a dog have a lot of hair?

PHIL: Most of them do.

TEACHER: What was another characteristic of a mammal?

And so on. Similarly, if learning a procedure means being able to name the procedure, to describe it, and to use it to solve problems, then your questions should get at each of those aspects of knowledge. Of course, unless you are doing one-on-one tutoring, you won't be able to limit your dialogue to one student—if you do so, then 23 other students in the class will punch their time cards and you and Phil will be on your own. You have to spread the questions around.

One problem with inquiry teaching is that to students it can seem like a game of academic keep-away. You have the information, but instead of sharing it with them you keep asking questions. You have to let them know that what you're attempting to teach is not the *answer* to a question, but the reasoning processes that go into *reaching* the answers.

The third alternative to showing the way is *discovery teaching*.[14] The essential idea of discovery teaching is to pose a problem (or take a problem posed by the student), and let the students work at it, either alone or in small groups. In practice, discovery teaching is *guided* discovery. A teacher might, for example, provide students with a sheet of paper on which there is a rectangular shape. She might note that the rectangle is 4 inches by 8 inches and then ask the students to determine the area.

The students, probably working in groups of three to five, would then be left to their own devices. After a few minutes, if a group has not discovered the solution, the teacher drops hints. She might, for example, give the students a set of one-inch blocks with the suggestion, "Maybe these will help." After several more minutes, if a group hasn't figured out the relationship between the blocks and the area, the teacher might hand each group a ruler and suggest that they mark off blocks of one square inch. If, after having done this, the students still haven't come up with the solution, the teacher might suggest that they count the number of squares marked off in the rectangle. And so on.

It is questionable whether the knowledge acquired through this process of progressive hints can be said to have been discovered, but this is what is meant by discovery teaching. It is, as you can imagine, far less efficient than simply saying to the students, "The way to compute the area of a rectangle is to multiply the length of an end by the length of a side."

J. E. Kittell demonstrated this decades ago when he gave some students a rule and had them apply it, and gave other students the opportunity to discover the rule.[15] He found that the students given a rule learned faster, retained more, and transferred what they learned to a new situation better than students who worked at discovering the rule. In fact, the students in the discovery group didn't learn much to retain or transfer. Other research has produced similar results.[16]

Meir Ben-Hur offers the example of Keith, a fifth grader who has just completed a four-month "hands on" science unit on planet Earth taught through the discovery method. An interview between Keith and the teacher went like this:

TEACHER: Where is the sun after it sets?

KEITH: I don't know. . . .

TEACHER (pointing to globes with labels hanging from ceiling and to student pictures on the wall): Is there anything in our classroom exhibit that can help you think about this?

KEITH (looking around): No. . . . But I know it doesn't go into the ocean.

TEACHER: How do you know that?

KEITH: Because it would splash the water.

TEACHER: Oh. So where does it really go?

KEITH (pausing): Maybe to China?[17]

As Keith's performance suggests, the evidence for discovery as an effective teaching method is weak. At best, learning is apt to be slow. Further, when students *do* discover something, it seems highly unlikely that an entire group will reach the Eureka! point simultaneously. As soon as one student discovers something, the rest of the class—or at least the rest of that's student's work group—is deprived of discovering it. The first student shares his or her discovery with others, thereby showing them the way.

Although discovery teaching is inefficient in the extreme, it is not entirely without value. For one thing, it offers a break from the normal routine, a different kind of challenge for the student than following where the teacher leads. Second, discovery teaching may have some motivational value. If, after a few moments, the students are unable to solve a problem, they may be eager to have a straightforward explanation from the teacher. This will satisfy the curiosity of some and relieve the frustration of others. Third, discovery teaching may help develop good problem-solving skills. One of the things students ought to be learning in school is how to tackle problems they have not encountered before. As noted earlier, these skills can be modeled the same as any others, but discovery gives the students the chance to practice them.

For example, when students are given the opportunity to examine bits of plants under a microscope, it is very unlikely that they will learn anything about plants that they couldn't learn more quickly from their teacher or a text. But they *can* learn how to use a microscope, how to examine objects at different magnifications, and how to draw and describe what they see. If they conduct an experiment to test the effects of different amounts of water on the growth of a plant, they get practice in designing an experiment, gathering data, and drawing conclusions. And they get to experience the pleasure of discovering something on their own, which is mostly why scientists conduct experiments.

The discovery method and inquiry teaching have some value and ought not to be banished entirely from the classroom. Even the lowly lecture can, on occasion, be worthwhile—if kept short. But these methods are far too inefficient to be the primary form of instruction. Most of the time, teachers should show the way.

Important as it is, showing the way is just the beginning of teaching. After showing the way, the teacher must . . .

Call for Action!

> *Whatever we learn to do, we learn by actually doing it.*
> —Aristotle

You can search high and low in the hallways of American schools, and you won't find one person to speak on behalf of passive learning. *Active learning* is the longest-surviving buzz phrase in education. Educators of every shape and stripe will argue with great vigor over school uniforms, the merits of basal readers, the optimum color for classroom walls, and whether geometry should come before or after algebra, but they will all calmly agree that students should be actively involved in the learning process. Passivity is taboo, verboten, outcast, forbidden.

Except, that is, in the classroom. There, the monastic rule of St. Benedict often still prevails: "It belongeth to the master to speak and to teach; it becometh the disciple to be silent and listen." As old fashioned and out of favor as the idea of passively sitting and listening to a teacher is, that is what passes for education a good deal of the time in many of our schools. In his now classic study of the history of American education, educational historian Larry Cuban found that across the decades, what a fly on the classroom wall was most likely to witness was a teacher talking and students sitting passively.[1] The assumption, of course, is that the students will (as good old St. Benedict dictated) keep their mouths shut and listen. The trouble is, that's not always—maybe not even usually—what happens.

What does happen is that the student's attention drifts. The result is what cognitive psychologist John Anderson and his colleagues call "attentional dropouts."[2] The student is there—he occupies a chair—but at some point during your lecture his brain checks out. (I suspect that as a student you were cognitively absent without leave a time or two yourself.) You can sometimes literally see this happening. The students scan the room, check out other students, peer out windows, count the number of holes in a square of ceiling tile. They are desperately looking for something—anything—more interesting, more intellectually stimulating than the drone of the master's voice. When Herb Childress sat in on high school classes for a year, what he saw, "mostly . . . was not learning at all but boredom."[3]

"But wait," you say, "didn't you just sing the praises of 'show and tell' instruction in a chapter not too far from here? Didn't you just say, basically, forget this idea of trying to teach the Pythagorean Theorem by giving students a problem to work on and then dropping 200-pound hints on them for 45 minutes until they finally 'discover' the solution? Just demonstrate it to them in two minutes and be done with it? Didn't I just read that? Well, didn't I?"

You did indeed, and I'm glad to see you were paying attention. However, I did not say that showing the way is the whole ball game or even the most important hitter in the lineup. It isn't. Teaching *begins* with showing the way, but for learning to occur, students must then *follow*. And to do that, they must act.

It is not enough, for example, to show a student how to make the printed letter "A," or to tell a student that an equation remains balanced if you subtract the same number from both sides. The student must then act on the information in some way. She might, for example, print the letter "A," or say "A" when a teacher points to that letter on a poster or in a book. The algebra student must try adding and subtracting numbers from both sides of an equation and see for himself that the two sides remain equal.

This is not, you will note, the same as saying the student must be active in some random way. Movement does not guarantee learning. Indeed, as Richard Anderson and Gerald Faust observed long ago, "Being 'active' and 'busy' are not enough. In fact, active responses which are irrelevant to the purpose of the lesson can interfere with learning."[4] We are not talking about aimless activity. We are talking about students attempting to perform something that they have just seen or heard.

It is an old idea for which John Dewey, the biggest name ever in American education, usually gets credit. Dewey said, "We learn by doing." This insight was actually arrived at a few years before Dewey by a Greek fellow with no first name called Aristotle, who said, "Whatever we learn to do, we learn by actually doing it." But Aristotle said it in ancient Greek, which may be why we give the point to Dewey, who had the good sense to say it in modern English.

Psychologists and educational researchers have repeatedly documented the wisdom of Dewey and Aristotle. In one of many studies, R. M. Travers and colleagues compared students who actively responded to a teacher's instruction with students who merely observed.[5] The active students learned more. Findings of this sort led Richard Anderson and colleagues to conclude decades ago that, "To be effective, all instruction must be accompanied by some form of active responding on the part of the student."[6] Just about everyone now agrees in principle (though quite a few people fall short in practice) that learning is not a spectator sport.

Despite the seeming consensus that active performance is necessary for optimal learning, there is some debate about what that means. Must the student perform overtly (calling out an answer or offering a comment, for example), or is it just as effective for him to respond covertly (by thinking of the answer or comment)? There's not much doubt that where motor skills are concerned, overt action is required. You can spend the entire day imagining that you are riding a bicycle, but it doesn't help much; you have to get on the bike to improve your riding skill.[7] Where academic learning is concerned, the evidence is more ambiguous, with some studies finding that overt responding gets better results and others showing that students learn just as much by performing "in their heads."

In the classroom, the point becomes moot, since we can't tell if students are performing unless they do so overtly. Suppose, after a brief explanation of parallel lines, I ask a group of students for a definition. I look out on the faces of the multitude, and I spy Sally Stitches and Hank Hitchens looking in my direction with beaming faces. Surely, I think, they are thinking, "Parallel lines are lines equidistant from one another at all points."

And that is, more or less, what Sally *is* thinking. Hank, on the other hand, is thinking, "It smells like they're making spaghetti in the cafeteria. I hope it has meatballs. Mmmm." Hank's body is with us, but his mind is out to lunch. His facial expression and body language belie the fact that he has become one of John Anderson's attentional dropouts.

Covert action may be every bit as good as overt action, but the teacher can't reliably tell when students are covertly performing as he'd like, and when they are cognitively absent. So the teacher's task is to get the students not just actively participating, but overtly participating. The problem then becomes: How do you get a student to do that?

The simplest way is to ask. Presented with a question, most students feel an obligation to attempt an answer. In answering they must act.

But what sort of question should you ask? Teacher questions are often classified into two types: lower-order and higher-order. Lower-order questions are those that can be answered simply by recalling some bit of information that has previously been presented. Examples of lower-order questions are:

- Who wrote the Gettysburg Address?
- What is the capital of Canada?
- When did Christopher Columbus reach the New World?
- How much is 7 plus 9?

There is usually only one, unambiguous, correct answer for lower-order questions, and that answer is usually expressed in one or two words. The answers to the questions above, for example, are Lincoln, Ottawa, 1492, and 16. If a student says Frederick Douglass wrote the Gettysburg Address, that the capital of Canada is Quebec, that Columbus arrived in 1066, that 7 and 9 are 79, we cannot say, "Ah, well, those are good answers, Georgie, but not precisely correct." They are not at *all* correct. They are totally, completely, and irrevocably *incorrect*, and there's no defending them. Furthermore, they can be proved to be wrong by logic, mathematical proof, or reference to an expert source such as an atlas or historical document.

Higher-order questions require the student to use information to draw inferences, make comparisons, give reasons, identify assumptions, and the like. While lower-order questions generally ask for information you've previously provided and nothing more, higher-order questions

FRANK & ERNEST: © Thaves/Dist. by Newspaper Enterprise Association, Inc.

most often require the use of provided information to analyze, integrate, or otherwise manipulate the information in order to arrive at new conclusions. Examples of higher-order questions include:

- What was Lincoln trying to accomplish in the Gettysburg Address?
- What are some of the similarities and differences between Ottawa and Washington, DC?
- How would America be different today if Columbus had turned back before reaching the Americas?
- How could you express the numbers 7 and 9 if you didn't use the base 10 numbering system?

Such questions usually require more than a few words to answer and often can have many, very good answers. Indeed, it is often hard to prove that an answer to such questions is incorrect. However, it is *not* the case that all answers to higher-order questions are equally good. Some are brilliant, some are mundane, and others are just plain rotten.

Just about everyone in America's schools of education takes it as a given that higher-order questions are better than lower-order questions. Most parents, on the other hand, seem to favor the lower-order questions. Judging by the kinds of questions teachers ask, most of them side with the parents, at least in practice.

The choice in the type of questions you ask depends partly on your notion of what education is all about. What are the goals? Is an educated person one who has accumulated a vast number of facts, or is an educated person one who can *make use of* facts?

Those who favor higher-order questions argue that simply being able to recite facts is of little practical value unless you get to be a contestant on *Jeopardy*. Otherwise, you can be replaced for $69.95, the price of the DVD version of the *Encyclopedia Britannica*. Those who favor lower-order questions fire back, "How are students going to deal with facts at a high level if they don't have any facts at hand? How are they going to talk about what Lincoln wanted to accomplish at Gettysburg if they haven't read the speech and don't know where Gettysburg is or why people gathered there? Sure, they can look that stuff up, but then you're acknowledging that facts are important. Besides, we can't look things up every time we want to think about something."

The defenders of higher-order questions worry that if facts are emphasized, students acquire only a shallow understanding of what they study. Only higher-order questions will get them deep into the subject matter, they insist. This argument sounds reasonable, but is not entirely supported by the facts. Nate Gage found, for example, that students do not show better understanding when teachers ask "thought" questions. "Indeed," he adds, "they have more often shown the reverse. Higher proportions of *lower*-order, or recall, questions have usually been accompanied by higher pupil scores on tests of both knowledge and understanding of the subject matter."[8] So it is not a slam dunk that asking a lot of low-level questions is going to turn students into fact bins with no real understanding of subject matter. Quite the contrary.

Still, it is hard to believe that asking thoughtful questions is a waste of time. After all, how can students *learn* to think about information if they are never *asked* to think about information?

It might be wise to emphasize factual questions in the early stages of learning and add thought questions as students acquire some familiarity with the subject. This would mean asking more lower-order questions in the early stages of studying the Gettysburg Address (which might require memorizing some or all of the address). Once they have studied the address and learned about the circumstances under which Lincoln gave it, students could then be challenged with more abstract questions about what Lincoln's words mean and what effect he hoped they would have.

It may be that higher-order questions are not terribly popular with teachers because they present certain difficulties. For one thing, the open-ended nature of thought questions means that in some subject areas they can lead to very controversial topics, including sex, contraception, abortion, the legalization of psychoactive drugs, homosexuality, gay marriage, and school prayer. By adolescence, most students are very interested in these topics, and many would like to wrestle with them in an honest, forthright way in our classrooms. But some parents get nervous when their children explore such topics, and nervous parents can make life difficult for teachers.

What's a teacher to do? Some teachers take the safe course and stick to factual questions. That may be good politics, but it's not necessarily in the best interest of the students. I think teachers do a better job when they include open-ended questions but select those questions based on the likely reaction of the phantom parent. The phantom parent is the parent you imagine sitting in the back of your class, listening attentively to everything you and your students say, and taking notes to read at the next Board of Education meeting. Any time you see the phantom parent taking notes, squinting, or squirming in his or her seat, you need to move to safer territory.

I know you would prefer that I give you concrete guidance, such as, "Never talk about sex" or "Avoid any discussion of the legalization of drugs." The trouble is, phantom parents are not all alike. A phantom parent in a private, college prep, nonsectarian school in Santa Barbara may be very different from one in a public, white-collar school in the suburbs of Indianapolis, or one in a public, inner-city, mostly minority school in Baltimore. And phantom parents in high schools are often less troubled by controversies than those in elementary schools. So you just have to get a feel for the phantom parent in your school. Talk to other teachers, talk to parents, go to some school-board meetings to see what parents are concerned about, and subscribe to and read the local newspaper in the town where you teach.

Some people will say that consulting phantom parents is cowardly. You should just teach to the best of your ability, they argue, and if that takes you into turbulent waters, so be it; the students have a right to explore whatever avenues of knowledge they choose. Besides, the hot topics are the ones that students find most interesting. Excise those topics and school becomes boring.

Personally, I'm not that idealistic. Teaching is tough enough without worrying about being tarred and feathered by angry parents. My view is that you do the best job you can within the limits set by the community. Sometimes the community will set limits that you will think make good sense. They don't want someone teaching kids how to use plastic explosives to blow something up, and neither do you. Sometimes the community sets limits you won't like. In that case you have to decide whether abiding by those limits does more harm than good. For my part, I will not teach students that the earth is flat, that the United States is always right, or that the Holocaust never happened. But I *will* steer students away from discussing topics that are not in the curriculum guide and are guaranteed to provoke a riot at the next PTA meeting. I can do my students a lot of good without inviting that kind of trouble, and I can't do them any good at all if I'm kicked out of the classroom.

How do you ask questions? Do you direct a question to the class at large and then choose from among the waving hands that appear? Or should you select your pigeon first, and then ask the question? Or would it be better to ask and then let someone call out an answer? You can probably find teachers who will defend any (or all) of these options, and perhaps others, but it is useful to consider the probable consequences of each.

If you ask a question and then accept the first good answer someone calls out, what will happen? The top students are going to call out answers, and the other students will find some other way to occupy their time, such as chatting with another student, passing notes, reading comic books, making strange noises, picking their noses—doing all the things kids do that endear them to teachers. You don't want that, so forget about having students call out answers.

"But what if the students *do* call out answers," you say, "even if I've told them not to?" They won't, if you don't hear them. Students call out answers to show off and win the teacher's approval. If the teacher ignores the called-out answer, calling out answers becomes pointless:

> TEACHER (pointing at the board): Is this a complete sentence, or is it a fragment?
>
> MARY (calling out): Fragment!
>
> TEACHER (looking out over a sea of hands): Let's see . . . Kang? Is this a sentence?
>
> KANG: It's a fragment.
>
> TEACHER: Right. A fragment. Who can tell me why it's a fragment?
>
> MARY (calling out): There's no verb!
>
> TEACHER: Melissa?
>
> MELISSA: It has a subject, but no verb.
>
> TEACHER: Correct!

It's true that Mary has given away the answers, and that Kang and Melissa may have answered correctly only because Mary already gave the answer away. So what? Besides, it won't be long before Mary gets the message. If she's slow to figure it out (unlikely, since she's bright enough to have the answers to your questions), you can mention to her in a quiet moment that although you like her to offer answers in class, she must do it the right way. She may pout a bit, but she'll soon raise her hand instead of calling out.

You will also find temporary deafness useful when you ask a question and half a dozen students, hands waving like pennants in the air, call out, "I know! I know!" If you call on someone else, even someone who *doesn't* know, then one of the know-it-alls will get quiet. When he does, call on *him*. Soon, the others will follow suit.

But wait a minute: Why do you object to students saying, "I know! I know! Pick me!" What's so terrible? We *say* we want students to be enthusiastic about learning, yet when they show any enthusiasm—laughing, or shouting "Wow! Look at that!" or calling out, "I know!"—we tighten the screws. "Try to contain yourself, Howard," we say. But how are kids supposed to show enthusiasm for learning? By sending us a postcard? Can you picture a third grader, or for that matter, a high school senior, smiling at you like Miss Marple and saying softly, "Oh, this lesson is ever so much fun. Yes, indeed." Can you imagine that? If you really believe that silence is golden, perhaps you should get a job as a fire spotter in a national forest. So, if you *like* the idea of students calling, "I know! I know," call on them. Maybe their enthusiasm will be contagious. Just make sure that you also call on students who are less enthusiastic. We want everyone to get into the act.

Selective deafness is also worth trying when the problem is that students call out silly answers:

> TEACHER (in a lesson on the American Revolutionary War): And why did Washington cross the Delaware? Yes, Barry?
>
> BARRY (looking especially pleased with himself): To get to the other side!

Such a comment, which seems to the teacher at best only slightly amusing, is apt to be hilarious to the average fifth grader, and to more than a few high school students. Many teachers make the mistake of responding to such silliness with a reprimand or sarcastic comment: "That's exactly the sort of infantile answer I would expect from you, Barry." This wins you no points with the students. Even if they agree with you, they probably expect you to act more grown up. And Barry is either humiliated, in which case he will seek revenge, or delighted to discover that he can push your buttons. When Barry offers a silly answer, I recommend selective deafness. Simply react as if Barry has said nothing at all, and call on another student.[9]

This raises another question about questions. Should you call only on students who want to answer? Many teachers feel they should. The students who don't raise their hands, they argue, obviously don't know the answer, so calling on them will just humiliate them. Often the teacher makes an unofficial pact with students who are in class in name only: Don't cause any trouble, and I won't call on you. I think this is a mistake that probably qualifies as educational malpractice. First, the students who don't raise their hands may know the answer more often than you think. If you never call on them, not only will you not discover your mistake, but the students will conclude that you assume they don't know anything, and how humiliating is that? Second, it is possible to ask even the slowest students questions they can answer. You can, for example, give students information and then immediately ask a question about that information:

> TEACHER: "Now we're going to read a speech called "The Gettysburg Address." What are we going to read, Richard?
>
> RICHARD: The Gettysburg Address.

If Richard gives you a blank stare in place of an answer, you can still get a good answer from him:

> RICHARD: I don't know.
>
> TEACHER: Martha, what's the title of the speech we're about to read?
>
> MARTHA: The Gettysburg Address.
>
> TEACHER: That's right, the Gettysburg Address. Richard, what's the name of the speech we're going to read?

RICHARD: The Gettysburg Address?

TEACHER: Very good.

Some teachers and parents object to this soft-glove approach. "You're spoon feeding them," they complain. "When they get in the real world, nobody is going to make it so easy for them." To which I say, Phooey! First, who says the classroom is not part of the real world? What is it, Disneyland? Second, my job as a teacher is not to create an environment that matches life outside of school in cruelty and hardship. It is to help every student learn as much as he or she can.

When kids are little, we cut up their meat for them. We don't give them a slab of beef and say, "Hey, deal with it! When you leave this cave, nobody's gonna cut up your meat for you." Our responsibility as teachers is to do what we have to do so that at the end of the day students can do more than they could do in the morning. So, we ask questions of all students, but we ask questions of the Reluctant Richards that we think they have a shot at answering.

Whatever kinds of questions you ask, you should spread them around. Teachers tend to call on certain students a lot and others hardly at all. One way to correct for this bias is to use a low-tech random number generator. For example, write students' names on bits of cardboard and put them into a jar. Ask a question and then draw a student's name from the jar. Throw the student's name back into the jar so that he or she can be called on at random again. An advantage to this system is that nobody feels picked on, or feels like you've saved all the tough questions for a few brainy students. The disadvantages are that it's cumbersome, and sometimes you end up asking a really tough question of a student who is not the sharpest tack in the shop.[10]

An alternative is to monitor your question-asking in some way. For example, you might have a seating chart and put a check mark in the box of a student each time you ask him or her a question. As the day progresses, you will realize you've asked five questions of Keisha and none of Joanne.

Another thing you can do to involve as many students as possible is ask the same question of different students:

TEACHER: How many sides does a triangle have, Jill?

JILL: Three?

TEACHER: Is that right, Marianne?

MARIANNE: Yes.

TEACHER: Really? Do you agree with that, Keiko?

FRED: Yes.

TEACHER: Harold?

HAROLD: Three sides.

TEACHER: Good. You're all correct.

In addition to involving more students, this tactic has the advantage of creating a certain tension. Students can't help wondering, "Is the teacher repeating the question because she's not getting the right answer? Could a triangle have more than three sides? Fewer?" The tension is relieved when the teacher acknowledges the answer is correct, and relief from tension makes an event memorable. If different students give conflicting answers, then this provides the opportunity to help students think through the problem:

TEACHER: How many sides does a triangle have, Jill?

JILL: Three?

TEACHER: Is that right, Marianne?

MARIANNE: I think you said that it has three or more sides.

TEACHER: Three or more sides. Do you remember when we said that the word triangle has two parts?

MARIANNE: Yes. Tri and angle.

TEACHER: Right. And we said that the prefix *tri* is used in other words, such as triathlon. Do you remember what a triathlon is?

MARIANNE: That's a competition with three different kinds of events, like swimming and running and biking.

TEACHER: So tri means . . .?

MARIANNE: Three.

TEACHER: So tri-angle means . . .?

MARIANNE: I get it. It means a figure with three sides.

Yet another way of involving more students is to make it possible for every student in the class to answer each question. It is now possible for students to have a sophisticated electronic device at each of their desks that allows them to answer a teacher's question by pressing a button or typing a reply. Each student's answer appears on a computer screen so that the teacher can monitor the class's progress and identify students who are having some trouble keeping up. No doubt this sort of technology will be available one day in all American classrooms. In the meantime, you can use a no-tech device that is more reliable, easier to use, and vastly cheaper. It's called the response card.

The response card is not exactly a new idea. In the days of the one-room school, they were made of a rectangular piece of slate. The deluxe model was smooth and had a wooden frame. These days the design has been improved somewhat by replacing the slate with a piece of whiteboard (the board used by presenters in workshops) and adding a handle, so the device looks like a rectangular Ping-Pong paddle.[11]

The teacher asks a question, and then the students write an answer on their paddles with an erasable marker and hold them up for the teacher to see. Now *every* student can answer. *Every* student can participate. *Every* student has something to do besides sit and listen. In addition, the teacher can scan the paddles and get a good idea how many pioneers she lost at the last turn in the academic road. And she can observe which students keep coming up with wrong answers and may need some extra help. It's difficult for students to see their classmates' answers, so embarrassment isn't much of a problem.

One thing to remember about asking a question is to give the student a chance to answer it. Although this is obvious, it is a principle that is commonly ignored. After asking a question, how long do you suppose teachers wait, on average, before turning to a different student or asking a different question? In other words, how much time do teachers give a student to start answering a question? (Take all the time you need to consider this question.)

Did you say 30 seconds? Hah! You jest! Ten seconds? You wish! Five seconds? No! The typical wait time (that is what this is called in "edspeak") is about one second.[12] One second! OK, some authorities say the average may be more like two or three seconds.[13] But still, can you believe it? Sit in on a class, and you will. If a student doesn't reply in the blink of an eye, the teacher asks another student the question, gives the answer, or asks a different question.

And it isn't just the pause after a question. Teachers are also quick of tongue after a student has made a reply. J. T. Dillon found that only about one in five teachers were silent for as much as three seconds after a student's comment.[14] In other words, students not only have to answer immediately, they also have to talk nonstop or their replies will be cut off.

Why are teachers so quick to hit the repeat button? I suspect there are two reasons. First, teachers are duty bound to teach the material in the curriculum guide, and the curriculum guide is crammed with stuff for students to learn. Fall behind today, and you've got more to teach tomorrow. Two or three days of that and you are hopelessly behind. So teachers often feel like they're in a kind of race. Sometimes they say as much to their students. "We don't have time to dawdle, Gertrude. We've got miles to go yet." It's push, push, push.

Second, in a conventional conversational setting, silence is not golden. It's more like poison ivy. We start to get uncomfortable when there is an empty space in a conversation. "Yes," you say, "but *one* second?" Try this experiment. The next time you're having a conversation with someone and it's your turn to speak, don't say anything. Take a quick look at the second hand on your watch and just sit there quietly for as long as you can. Chances are good you won't last five seconds. And if you last longer than five seconds, the chances are your partner won't. He or she will make another comment, or ask a question—perhaps, "Is something wrong?" Now you understand why the teacher who asks a question usually feels uncomfortable after two or three seconds of silence, even if the student seems to be preparing to answer.

It's really too bad, because increasing the wait time gives a student time to ponder the question and compose a reasonable reply. We *say* we want students to be thoughtful. Well, then we should give them time to think. Increasing wait time results in more answers and better answers. If you ask a student a question that requires more than a one- or two-word reply, give her a few seconds to gather her thoughts and a few more seconds after she answers, in case she wants to add a footnote.

A little more wait time can be useful even when answering requires only recalling some fact. It doesn't take a lot of time to answer the question, "Who invented the lightbulb?" But a student who hasn't quite got that factoid firmly etched in his or her memory module may need to ruminate about it for a few seconds. Ruminating is good. Ruminating is how we pull things up to the surface, including things that we know, such as who invented the lightbulb or where we left our car keys.

Increasing wait time does, however, slow the pace of instruction. Some teachers think that the ideal pace is rapid fire: question-answer, question-answer, question-answer, bing, bing, bing. Move right along. No time to get bored, no time to get sleepy, everybody's active, everybody's learning. There *is* a positive correlation between the number of questions asked and the amount of learning.[15] And, as mentioned earlier, lower-level questions (those that focus on recall of facts) do seem to improve learning, not just in recall of facts but in understanding and application. So a good case can be made for the idea that a fast pace means more learning—and that means short wait times.

The other side of that educational coin is that one of the things we want students to do is deal with questions in a thoughtful, methodical way, and they can only learn to do that if we give them time to be thoughtful and methodical. So, what should the pace be, Maserati fast or tugboat slow?

Once again, the best approach is probably the middle road—which is to say, not somewhere between the Maserati and the tugboat, but a combination of the two. Vary the pace. You can do this by interspersing thoughtful questions here and there among the recall items. You can also do it by matching the kinds of questions you ask to the mood of the class. When students are alert and attentive, ask a mind bender. When they are starting to get sluggish, bring on the short-answer questions: bing, bing, bing.

Of course, the proportion of thoughtful questions will also vary with the students you teach and the subject. If you are teaching beginning reading, you probably should ask a higher proportion of recall questions than you would ask of high school students taking advanced-placement English.

So, to review: Ask a lot of questions, ask a variety of questions, and give students time to reply—especially to thoughtful questions. If a student can't answer or answers incorrectly, back up and ask a question he or she can answer and build on that (à la Socrates) to get to the original question.

Questions are probably the most important tool a teacher has for getting students actively involved in learning, but they are not the only tool. Two other commonly used tools for inducing action are direction and physical guidance.

Usually we can easily induce students to perform by simply directing them to do so:

> TEACHER (after writing the word *establishment* on the board): See if you can sound out this word . . . John.
>
> JOHN: Es-tab-lish-ment.
>
> TEACHER: Good. Establishment. Everybody say, *es-tab-lish-ment.*
>
> CLASS: Es-tab-lish-ment.
>
> TEACHER: Fine. Say *establishment.*
>
> CLASS: Establishment.
>
> TEACHER: Excellent.

Physical guidance consists of inducing students to perform an action by actually moving them through the action. It is often used after modeling. You model a skill and then physically guide students as they attempt to imitate your demonstration. For example, while modeling the proper grip on a golf club, you ask a student to hold a club in the same way. If his grip is not right, you move his fingers into the appropriate position. When you move his fingers, you are using physical guidance.

Physical guidance is used a good deal in teaching sports skills and it comes in handy in art and music instruction, but it also serves the teacher well in teaching academic skills. When children are first learning to wield a pencil, for example, they often need some help with their grip. Later, the child who writes b for d and vice versa might be helped to learn the difference by guiding her hand as she grips the pencil. It helps for the teacher to exaggerate the key movements and describe what is happening. For example:

> Let's make a "b." We move the pencil down the page to make a flag-pole (the teacher covers the student's hand with her own and helps him move appropriately), and now we go back up a bit and we move the pencil to the *right* (said while leaning the child's hand far to the right) and down, and now back to the flagpole. Now let's make "d." We make another flagpole, like so, then we come up a little bit, and now we push the pencil to the *left* (again leaning the hand far to the side), and down, and back to the pole.

A more subtle way of directing students to perform is to make a deliberate mistake. I talked in the last chapter about foolers as a way of demonstrating the difference between correct and incorrect facts and procedures. Foolers are also a way of getting students to act on what they have learned.

By using physical guidance, foolers, directions, and especially questions, you can induce students to act on the information you have provided. Once the students have acted, you need to let them know how they did—you need to . . .

Give Feedback

> *The simplest prescription for improving education must be "dollops of feedback."*
> —John Hattie

Modern technology has its virtues. When the winter winds blow, I am glad that I don't have to go outside and fetch wood to throw into a stove. I simply set my thermostat to the desired temperature. When the air temperature in my home falls, the thermostat sends a signal to the furnace that turns it on. When the air temperature rises to the desired level, the thermostat sends a signal to the furnace that turns it off. In a sense, the job of the thermostat is to tell the furnace how it is performing.[1] Engineers call this sort of information *feedback,* a word that means input *to* a machine based on output *from* that machine.

The feedback concept has migrated to fields outside of engineering. In education it means input *to* a student based on output *from* that student. In both education and engineering, feedback implies a loop. Performance triggers feedback, which in turn triggers a change in performance, which triggers feedback, which triggers a change in performance, and so on.

There is, however, an important difference between the two cases. In engineering, the purpose of feedback is usually to maintain a steady performance (the "goal" of the thermostat, for example, is to get the furnace to maintain a nearly constant room temperature). In education, the goal of feedback is to improve performance. That point is worth repeating. The purpose of instructional feedback is *not* to *maintain* the student's current level of performance, but to *improve* it.

There are two types of instructional feedback, positive and negative. Positive feedback tells students what they did right (or, at least, better than before). Negative feedback tells students what they did wrong (or not as well as before).

Examples of positive feedback include statements such as *right, good, well done, excellent, nice job, well said,* and more detailed comments, such as "You held the racket just right," "Good. You remembered to put a comma before the conjunction," and "I know these problems are difficult, and I'm glad to seeing you're sticking with them." Positive feedback also includes such nonverbal gestures as the nod of a head, a smile, applause, a thumbs-up sign, and a congratulatory handshake.[2]

Examples of negative feedback include statements such as *wrong, bad, no, not good,* "You shouldn't bend your elbow," "You forgot to put a comma before the conjunction," and "After all this time you've solved only one problem?" Negative feedback also includes nonverbal gestures such as a squinted eye, a frown, a thumbs-down sign, and a sneer.

Of course, positive and negative feedback can both be offered following a performance. The struggling math student might be told, for instance, "You're on the right track, but your calculations are wrong." Now he knows that his strategy is correct, and he knows where to look to get the correct answer. Combining information about what the student has done well and where he erred is likely to produce the most rapid rate of learning.

Today, most educators recognize that feedback is an extremely powerful teaching tool. This has not always been so. Prior to 1900, repetition was often considered sufficient for learning. Then researchers began doing experiments that revealed that practice by itself was usually of limited value. It was feedback that made practice worthwhile. In one experiment, E. L. Thorndike, the founder of educational psychology, asked students to draw a four-inch line while blindfolded. He gave some students feedback on their performance. If their line was within 1/8 inch of the standard, he said "Right." If it was off by more than 1/8 inch, he said "Wrong." Although this feedback was very crude, these students improved substantially, while students who got no feedback at all made no progress.[3]

Drawing a line of a certain length is, of course, a trivial skill, but research confirms that feedback plays a huge role in classroom learning as well.[4] By 1951, Dael Wolfe could write, "Laboratory studies are unequivocal in emphasizing the importance of giving a subject as specific and as immediate information as possible concerning the outcome of his efforts."[5] The value of feedback in teaching was so well established by 1989 that Donald Kauchak and Paul Eggen wrote, "The value of practice and feedback in improving learning is one of the most consistent findings from the teacher effectiveness literature."[6] And in 1992, John Hattie concluded, "The most powerful single modification that enhances achievement is feedback. The simplest prescription for improving education must be 'dollops of feedback.'"[7]

But you don't need to read research to know that feedback is a powerful tool. Chances are you saw a clear demonstration of it long ago—though you might not have realized it—when you played the children's game, *Hot and Cold*. In this game, a child is to find (i.e., learn the location of) a hidden object, based solely on feedback from others about whether she is getting closer or farther away. As the child moves toward the object, others call out, "You're getting warmer." As she moves away from the object, others cry, "You're getting colder." Gradually the seeker gets closer and closer to the goal, until finally she reaches it.

I have had many college students play a version of this game, which I call the Teaching Game, in order to show them the extraordinary power of even simple, unsophisticated feedback.[8] First I have the students teach me. While I am out of the room, the students discuss what they want me to do. There are certain limitations. Given the time constraints, it can't be too complicated, and it shouldn't be anything embarrassing, such as sitting on a student's lap, or dangerous, such as trying to do a handstand.

When the students have decided on a goal, they invite me to return. Then they try to teach me whatever it is they want me to do. They might want me to approach a particular student and offer to shake his hand, or they might want me to stand on my right foot and put my left hand on my head. They have only one tool at their disposal—positive feedback. Whenever I do anything that moves me closer to the goal, they say *yes*. For example, if they want me to stand on my right foot, then when I shift my weight to my right foot, they yell (and they *do* yell), *yes!* If I lift my left foot off the floor very slightly, they yell *yes* again. They cannot offer instructions, they cannot model or describe the behavior they want, they cannot provide negative feedback (such as saying *no*) when I do something inappropriate. Their only tool is a primitive form of positive feedback—saying *yes* whenever I make some slight progress toward the goal.[9]

It seems an impossible task, yet the students typically shape the behavior they want within three minutes. The results are so impressive that sometimes the "teachers" cannot believe it. Once the goal was to get me to walk over to a wall map, pull the map away from the wall, and stand behind it. I had no idea what the goal was, and simply did whatever produced yeses, but in less than 30 seconds I was standing against the wall, hidden by the map. The students erupted in self-congratulatory applause. Sometime after this, I had the students complete an anonymous course evaluation and one student complained, "I know we didn't really get you to stand behind that map!" The effects of feedback were so powerful that this student was convinced some sort of trickery must have been involved.

After demonstrating the effects of positive feedback, I then ask for a volunteer for a new demonstration. (I have no trouble getting volunteers once I have served as a volunteer myself.) The volunteer leaves the room, the class decides on a new challenge, and we proceed as before. The student learns quickly, and I ask her to try another challenge. This time, however, I ask the class to rely solely on negative feedback, saying *no* whenever the student does something other than what they want. For example, if the task is to stand on the right foot, then each time the student shifts her weight to her *left* foot, they say *No*. The students are amazed at how slowly learning proceeds with negative feedback. Indeed, there is often no progress at all. The student who had just seemed so bright now seems positively dense. The difference, of course, is not in the student, but in the kind of feedback provided.[10]

In addition to the fact that positive feedback usually results in faster learning, it also tends to uplift and motivate, whereas negative feedback tends to depress and demoralize. This is not to say that all feedback needs to be positive. Pointing out where a student has gone astray is not only helpful, but sometimes essential. But if most feedback is negative, the prevailing mood is negative. To use 1960s language, negative feedback produces negative "vibes." The vast majority of feedback a teacher provides should be positive.

The effectiveness of feedback—positive or negative—varies greatly, depending on its characteristics. To be most effective, feedback should be honest, unambiguous, immediate, specific, brief, corrective, and frequent.

Effective feedback is honest. Feedback isn't feedback if it isn't an honest reaction to a student's performance. Passing out praise like party favors is not feedback at all, and it is very unlikely to result in improvement. When you say something about a student's work, you and the student should both know that you are telling the truth, that the comment is really deserved. This is true whether the feedback is positive or negative.

This does not mean, however, that you should offer positive feedback only when the student meets some arbitrary standard. You may object that this means offering false praise, which is hardly honest. But that is not what I'm suggesting. I'm saying that the most important standard should be progress. If a student writes a one-page story that includes 12 spelling errors, I can still say, "You had three fewer spelling errors than last time, Bob. Way to go!" Or you can combine honest negative feedback with honest positive feedback, as in, "You had a lot of spelling mistakes, Katy, but I noticed you spelled 'receive' correctly; you used to get that wrong." Progress, however slight, is worth noticing and commenting on. And if there has been no progress in spelling, I might say, "I had some trouble reading your story because of the spelling errors, but I enjoyed it. It was very funny." This combines negative and positive feedback, and both are honest.

Effective feedback is unambiguous. One reason the Teaching Game works so well is that there is nothing ambiguous about *yes.* When you hear *yes,* you know that you have done something right. You may not know what you've done right (you can only expect so much information from a three-letter word), but you know you've done *something* correctly. Of course, there's no magic in the word *yes.* You could just as easily say *right, better* or, for that matter, *cucumber.* As long as students understand that when they hear *cucumber,* it means they have done something right, you will see progress.

Unfortunately, the feedback students get in their classes is not always that clear cut. Teachers often reply to a student answer or comment with "OK." Does OK mean, "That's correct," "I hear what you're saying," or something else? Generally speaking, "OK" is open to interpretation. So are "Hmmmmm," "Uh-huh," "Could be," "I see," "Ah . . ." "Maybe," and "Interesting comment." If you want to convey to students that they have got something right or made a perceptive observation, these comments aren't going to do the job. Yet a study by David and Myra Sadker of 4th, 6th, and 8th grade classrooms revealed that more than half of all teacher comments were of this type, more than all other types of teacher comments combined. "In analyzing thousands of teacher reactions," the authors write, "the 'O.K.' or 'un-huh' type of response was far and away the most common."[11] Unfortunately, these kinds of comments have little or no value as feedback.

Some feedback becomes ambiguous when we qualify a comment. Consider Bill, a less-than-stellar student who seldom makes much of an effort. When he does exert himself, he usually performs poorly. What do you say when he gets something right? You could say much the same thing you might say to any other student, something like, "That's right, Bill. Very good." Unfortunately, some teachers will say, "Congratulations, Bill. You finally got something right." Saying, "You *finally* got something right" is positive feedback put through a meat grinder. It turns success into failure. In my view, there is no place for such sarcasm in the classroom. Hurtful remarks often cause far more pain than teachers realize. They demoralize the student and often inspire retaliation, sometimes in the form of "senseless" mischief. The sting of nasty comments from a teacher can sometimes endure for decades.

I've never heard of a student being helped by sarcasm. People say, "Never say never." Well, I'm making an exception: When you provide feedback, *never* be sarcastic. If a student does something praiseworthy, praise the behavior and let it go at that. Don't pat her on the back and then push her down a flight of stairs.

Effective feedback is immediate. Feedback should occur during the student's performance, or as soon thereafter as possible. Although learning to ride a bike often involves cuts and bruises, the human gyroscope works remarkably well, and we usually improve quickly. One reason for this is that the feedback we get is instantaneous. Lean a bit too far to one side and you immediately feel impending doom. Shift your weight and you immediately feel more secure.

The student in a classroom, by contrast, writes an essay or takes a spelling test and a week later gets "feedback." Can you imagine learning to ride a bicycle if the signals from your middle ear were delayed by, say, 10 seconds? It would be almost impossible. Yet the feedback we offer in school usually comes days and sometimes weeks after the student's performance.

In World War II, soldiers in the U.S. Army Signal Corps learned to send and receive Morse code. In this system, combinations of short and long sounds (called "dots" and "dashes") represent letters and numbers. The letter W, for example, is represented by dot-dot-dash, while P is dot-dash-dash-dot. Part of the soldier's task was to be able to hear the dots and dashes and write down the correct letter or number. It took 35 to 40 hours of training before soldiers could decode five words per minute. Then Fred Keller modified the instruction so that the soldiers got immediate feedback.[12] The instructor would send a signal, such as dot-dash-dash-dot, then pause for two or three seconds while the soldiers wrote down the letter or number represented. Then the instructor called out the correct answer. No other feedback was provided. The result of this simple change in procedure was that soldiers reached the five-words-per-minute rate of decoding in about 10 fewer hours. Perhaps more important, only about 3% of the soldiers ultimately failed to meet the standard, compared to 15% with the older method. Immediate feedback made the difference.[13]

I have used the Teaching Game to show students the effects of delayed feedback. I ask a student to serve as guinea pig, and while that student is out of the room, the other students decide what they want to teach him to do. Before the student returns to class, however, I make a new rule. The "teachers" are to count to three before saying *yes*. With this short delay, learning progresses much more slowly and is a frustrating ordeal for the student. After several minutes of little or no progress, I then have the student leave the room while we think up another task for him. When he returns, the teachers provide immediate feedback. The contrast is extraordinary. The "stupid" student is suddenly brilliant.

Feedback delays are sometimes inevitable, but they are to be avoided whenever and wherever possible. If you want to produce the most learning, offer feedback immediately. There are many ways to do this. For example:

- Have each student give a short speech before four other students and then hear what their audience thought of it.
- Ask students to exchange essays and look for specific flaws (such as pronoun reference errors).
- After students take a test, collect their papers and immediately discuss the answers item by item.

And so on. Any reduction in the delay of feedback makes feedback more effective.

Effective feedback is specific. Feedback should clearly specify the aspects of the student's performance that are being commented on. An unambiguous yes or no is useful feedback, but it tells the student only that he did something right or wrong. The student is then left to figure out what, exactly, was right or wrong. It's nice to hear someone say, "Good job," but it's far more helpful to know what was good about the job. For example, a soccer coach might tell a player during practice that he has done well. But look at the difference between, "Good job, John!," and "Good passing, John!" In the first instance, John knows he did well. In the second, John knows *what* he did well. The student who is writing an essay might be told, "This article is very well written." The student will no doubt be pleased to hear it, but she will be helped a lot more by hearing, "Your opening sentence is very good; it really made me want to read the article."

Negative feedback should also be specific. "You went off on a tangent in the third paragraph, and that weakened your essay" is much more helpful than "Your essay wasn't very good," or even "Your discussion wandered."

The superiority of specific feedback over general feedback has been demonstrated many times. M. H. Trowbridge and H. Cason replicated Thorndike's line drawing experiment.[14] Some students got no feedback, some were told "right" or "wrong" (depending on how far off their line was), and some were given detailed information about the length of each line. After 100 trials, those who got no feedback drew lines that were off by almost an inch, on average; those who got vague feedback ("right" or "wrong") were off by about half an inch; and those who got specific feedback were off by about one-tenth of an inch. The same results occur when classroom learning is involved. Specific feedback produces more improvement than general feedback does.

Effective feedback is brief. Being specific often requires more than a one-word comment, but feedback should not be any wordier than necessary. The problem with long-winded feedback is the same as the problem with long lectures. Even though more information is provided in a longer version, it tends to be lost on the student.

When I was a young and foolish English teacher, I conscientiously bled red ink over hundreds of student essays. I pointed out, if not every error I could find, at least enough errors to convince the best of my students that there was no hope of them ever becoming competent writers. I eventually realized that my good intentions had wasted a lot of my time and done my students little good. I would have had far more leisure time in the evening, and my students would have been far better served, if I had limited myself to identifying the most egregious one or two errors in each student's paper.[15]

By limiting the amount of feedback, I would have had a better chance of focusing my students' attention on the one or two things they most needed to do to improve. And by being more sparing in my negative comments, the students might have noticed that I had a few *positive* things to say about their work.

Effective feedback is corrective. Students want and need feedback that tells them what they can do to improve. Positive feedback usually tells them this, since it identifies something they did right, but negative feedback often tells the student only what *not* to do. However, it is usually possible to phrase negative feedback in a more constructive way. For example, you could say to a student, "Your essay wasn't convincing because you gave only one reason for your position." Or you could say, "You gave a good reason for your position, but your essay will be more convincing if you offer a few more reasons." Instead of saying, "You're holding the bat too high" you can say, "Try holding the bat lower." Instead of, "You spoke too softly," say, "If you speak more loudly, people in the back will be able to hear you better."

In each case, both statements point out a flaw in the student's performance, but the second versions do it in more positive ways. Such state-

"This note from your mother is a forgery. . . .
But your penmanship is better than usual."

George B. Abbott

ments focus students' attention on what they need to do to improve, rather than on how they failed. When negative feedback is offered in this more agreeable way, it is often called corrective feedback.

M. C. Elawar and L. Corno compared the effects of two kinds of feedback on sixth grade students learning mathematics.[16] Some students got papers returned with items marked either right or wrong. Other students' papers included praise for something they did right and suggestions for improving their performance. The two groups of students had similar scores on a pretest, but those who received praise and suggestions for improvement learned about twice as much during the study. These students also enjoyed math more than students who got less feedback.

Effective feedback is frequent. Generally speaking, the more often a student's efforts are followed by feedback, the faster the student progresses.[17] Note that we are talking now about frequency, not amount. It is far better to provide brief feedback after every student effort than to provide detailed feedback after one of every ten performances.

Unfortunately, research indicates that in the typical American classroom, feedback is far from frequent.[18] Sadker and Sadker studied teacher feedback in fourth, sixth, and eighth grade classrooms.[19] They found that clear feedback, both positive and negative, was rare. Positive feedback occurred after only 11% of student efforts. In one-fourth of classes, the teacher never provided positive feedback.[20] The frequency of feedback is low in the lower grades and becomes even less common as the students grow older. Feedback, arguably the most powerful tool available to the teacher, is largely absent from high school classrooms.

Not only is feedback provided infrequently, it is distributed unequally. Sadker and Sadker found that a small group of students received a large share of the feedback, while 25% of students never received any feedback.[21]

Teachers are typically disbelieving when presented with such findings. They think that they spend a lot of time giving feedback to all their students. If you find yourself among the disbelievers, try this: Put a tape recorder on your desk and turn it on. Record your classes for at least a day, then tally the number of times you provided feedback to each student. Chances are good that you will be embarrassed by the results.

One way teachers can get themselves to provide more feedback and distribute it more equitably is to put a check mark on the seating chart next to each student's name whenever they provide feedback. They can also encourage their students to ask for feedback, especially those students who tend to be neglected.

But no teacher, however conscientious, can provide all the feedback needed by 20 or 30 students. Fortunately, there are other sources of feedback besides the teacher. There are, for example, natural forms of feedback. The Japanese say, "The bow teaches the archer," meaning that the natural feedback we get from performing a skill helps us learn it. In the same way, students can sometimes get some natural feedback about their classroom performance. When learning to type, for example, you don't need to be told you hit the right key—you can see it on the computer monitor.

Teacher aides are another source of feedback. During an exercise, an aide can move about the room, checking student work and commenting on good points and mistakes. In checking written work, the bias is toward pointing out errors, so it may be a good rule of thumb for the aide to make *at least* one positive comment for every negative comment. Of course, teachers should also follow the same guideline.

Another important source of feedback is the students themselves. In peer tutoring, one student who has mastered a skill tries to help another who is struggling to learn it. A student could, for example, attempt to solve a problem while the tutor observes and tells him when he is on target and when he goes astray.

I have often used a slightly different approach that I call pair learning. In pair learning, neither student is identified as a tutor. Instead, the pair work together to solve a problem or master a skill. One student may practice giving a short speech while the other listens and provides feedback. Then the students trade roles. The same thing can be done with groups of three to five. Students are often quite good at giving feedback. A teacher may have trouble understanding why a student finds a skill difficult to acquire, but a student who recently learned the skill herself knows what the hurdles are, and how to clear them.

Since the power of feedback varies with the credibility of the source, feedback from students is often less effective than that from teachers. However, sometimes student feedback can be more powerful than a teacher's. Some teachers allow students to write notes and "mail" them to other students in the class. When a student writes a note and gets the reply, "I can't read what you wrote," from another student, he is probably more inclined to work on improving his handwriting than he would be if his teacher made the same complaint.

Students can also provide feedback to themselves. Psychologists have found that simply keeping track of one's performance is an excellent way of improving it. A student who is a slow reader, for instance, might record the number of words per minute that she reads at the end of each daily practice session. It helps if the student plots the data on a graph, since the slope of the line shows the amount of progress and is great feedback.

Learning materials can be designed to provide feedback. Textbooks and workbooks make feedback available when they enable students to check the answers. Computers do this more efficiently, and they can ensure that the student solves the problem *before* looking at the answer.

Sophisticated computer simulations can provide detailed feedback about certain kinds of performance. For example, at the American Sports Medicine Institute in Birmingham, baseball pitchers hurl balls while being filmed. The information is fed into a computer, which then reveals what a pitcher does well and what needs improvement. One day, such high-tech feedback may be available to help children learn to read or play the violin.

Teachers need to make use of as many different sources of feedback as they can in order to increase the "dollops of feedback" students get. When feedback is used properly, students usually learn quickly. For students to retain what they have learned, and become even more skilled, we must . . .

Provide Practice, Practice, and More Practice

"Let's try it again," Sullivan said, over and over: "Let's try it again." Then, finally, "Good." And they began practicing outside loops.
    —Richard Bach, *Jonathan Livingston Seagull*

In the fantasy film *Dinotopia,* the timid David is told that his lifework is to fly the huge stork-like creatures called pteranadons. David, who is afraid of heights and shows no talent for pilot work, is a reluctant recruit. He climbs aboard a pteranadon simulator, a device that gyrates and spins like a rodeo bull, and is soon thrown to the ground. He tries again and is again thrown to the ground. Again and again he climbs onto the simulator and is thrown off. Finally he manages to hold on, and eventually he masters the task and earns his pilot wings.[1]

I suspect that most viewers of the movie applaud David's perseverance and have no trouble believing that he could reach his goal through dogged practice. But within American education, there are many who believe that long practice, or maybe any practice at all, is pointless and even harmful.[2] Their mantra is "drill and kill," meaning that practice does nothing for students but kill their interest in learning.

I don't agree. Instead of "drill and kill," I believe "drill and instill" would be more accurate. Critics of practice may call me an antiquarian, a drillmaster, or worse. Perhaps, but I believe in practice, by which I mean any repetitive performance, including (but not limited to) the use of flash cards, worksheets, recitation, choral drill, songs, rereading, computer games, and pteranadon and other simulators. I say this without apology because I think the benefits of practice are beyond question. Those benefits include improved performance, retention, and transfer.

Practice improves performance. Someone once asked a professional golfer if luck played any role in his success. "Absolutely," he said, "and the more I practice, the luckier I get." Most of us readily accept the idea that practice is important to success in skilled sports. We know that top ice skaters, gymnasts, and golfers spend many long hours practicing for several years (and sometimes decades) before they achieve outstanding performance. What many people don't realize is that the same thing is true in the acquisition of academic knowledge and skills.

Benjamin Bloom and K. Anders Ericsson, working separately, studied the development of expertise in a variety of areas, including not only sports, art, and music, but also cognitive domains such as writing, mathematics, and scientific research. Both found that what distinguishes experts from others is not exceptional innate capacity, but years of study and "deliberate practice."[3] Even those recognized as geniuses required ten years or more of intense study and practice before doing the highest level

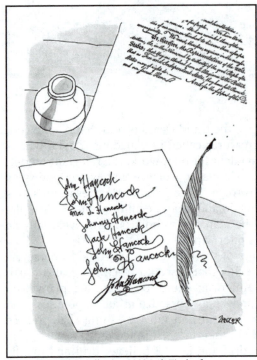

of work.[4] Mozart, for example, though famous for writing a symphony at age eight, did not write music considered high caliber until he was about 16. That is very young, to be sure, but by that time he had devoted many hours a day *for 12 years* to the systematic study and practice of music.

Even fairly simple skills benefit from practice. For example, conventional medical training in the use of a stethoscope to identify abnormal heart sounds usually consists of a lecture and playing a couple of recordings of the sounds. Michael Barrett, a cardiologist at Temple University, found that after such training third-year medical students correctly identified abnormal heart sounds only 39% of the time.[5] With additional practice using simulated heart sounds, their success rate jumped to 89%, about as good as most practicing cardiologists. But achieving this high level of skill required listening an average of 500 times to each of six abnormal heart sounds.

If simple skills require extensive practice, it is absurd to suggest that people can master complex skills such as reading, writing, and math, or acquire large knowledge bases in areas such as science and history, without extensive practice. Practice may not make perfect, but it definitely improves performance.

Practice improves retention. People say that once you learn to ride a bicycle you never forget, but it's not entirely true. In fact, knowledge and skill begin to deteriorate as soon as we cease practicing. If you stop riding a bicycle at age 12, 20 years later you may manage to stay on board a bike but you won't ride with the same facility you had decades earlier. We recognize this fact when we do poorly at a skill and say, "I'm out of practice."

Practice does not guarantee retention, but it builds up a kind of reserve so that forgetting occurs more slowly. Harry Bahrick has spent his entire career studying the retention of classroom learning. What he has found is that how well people remember depends largely on how long they study.

For instance, Bahrick studied people who had learned Spanish in high school but had not used the language afterwards. The amount of forgetting depended on how many years of Spanish the former students had completed. Those who had completed only one year of Spanish forgot essentially everything they had once known within three to five years. Those who completed three years of study retained about 29% of what they knew when they completed their studies. Those who studied Spanish for five years retained 63% of what they had learned.[6]

Sixty-three percent may not sound particularly impressive, but keep in mind that these students did not, after leaving school, make significant use of Spanish in their daily lives. Those who studied Spanish for five years forgot a third of what they had known fairly quickly, but after that they forgot very little for the next *50 years*.

Prolonged practice, Bahrick suggests, puts knowledge into *permastore*, "content that is maintained for several decades without benefit of additional rehearsal."[7] It becomes so well established, we could say it is anchored in the brain. Studies on forgetting in other subjects tell a similar story.[8] Most of what we practice for a short time is forgotten. Most of what we practice for a long time can stay with us for decades.

Bahrick's studies do not separate instruction from practice, per se, but it is clear that if a person studies Spanish for five years, he or she must get a great deal more practice than the student who studies for only one year. The conclusion is inescapable that if we want students to retain what they learn, then we must ensure that they get lots of practice.

Practice improves transfer. You will recall that the word *transfer* means the tendency for learning that occurs in one situation to carry over to new situations.[9] Many teachers expect students to learn things in one situation and then apply them in other situations automatically. They believe that if students can just be made to *understand* a fact, principle, or procedure, they will easily apply it wherever and whenever it is applicable. Unfortunately, as transfer expert J. Ronald Gentile and others have pointed out, this sort of "spontaneous transfer" happens a lot less than teachers think.[10]

In fact, to get transfer you have to teach for transfer. One of the best ways to do that is—you guessed it—practice. Experts of various theoretical orientations (including cognitive and behavioral) now generally agree that learning is anchored to the context in which it occurs. In order for what the students learn in one context to carry over to other contexts, they must practice in a variety of contexts. It follows that the more situations in which a skill is practiced or knowledge is used, the more likely it is to transfer to new situations.

Transfer is also aided by expertise. The more a student knows about a topic, the more likely he is to make use of what he knows in a variety of situations. As Gentile puts it, "Learners must develop a rich knowledge base and master, to near automaticity, basic skills."[11] And how do students master basic skills "to near automaticity"? Through practice.

If you want students to spell words correctly, not only on the spelling tests but in other situations, they must practice spelling the words correctly in other situations. For instance, instead of having the students write a word three times, have them write three different sentences that include the word. And ask them to work each of their spelling words into things that they write during the week—essays, poems, stories, speeches, answers to science or history questions.

You could also give students printouts of stories or essays that include some of the spelling words but contain blanks where the spelling words should appear. The students' assignment is not merely to read the material for the usual purposes, but to write in the missing words. You might also ask a student now and then to spell aloud one of that week's spelling words.

I have argued (successfully, I hope) that practice improves performance, retention, and transfer. To get the most benefit out of practice, it must meet certain criteria.

Practice should be informed. To get the maximum benefit from practice, it must include feedback about performance. This is called *informed practice*. Uninformed practice can even make performance *worse*. In a study during World War II, for example, Donald Lindsley found that radio operators who did not receive feedback about their performance actually became *less* accurate with practice.[12] One reason for the adverse effects of practice without feedback is probably that as mistakes creep into performance, those mistakes get practiced.[13]

Ideally, students should practice under the supervision of an expert, such as the teacher, but that is often impossible. Fortunately, less-than-ideal feedback is readily available and often highly effective. For instance, students can pair off and take turns repeatedly reading passages aloud; while one student reads, the other student listens and provides feedback. This has been shown to improve reading rate, accuracy, and comprehension.[14] Students can also pair off and practice spelling words aloud; they can give speeches to small groups of students who then offer critiques; they can solve a math problem and then check their work by looking in the back of a book or by consulting a "solution card" provided by the teacher; they can practice on a computer program that provides a point each time they perform correctly.[15]

The value of feedback during practice may seem obvious, but the most obvious thing about it is that its importance is often ignored.[16] As noted in chapter 5, teachers do not always provide feedback as frequently as they should. In addition, certain instructional procedures preclude feedback. For example, children are routinely asked to learn their weekly spelling words by writing each word three times. They do so with the correct spelling in front of them, and they are thus not so much *spelling* the word as *copying* it. If they cover the word, write it, and *then* check their work, they are getting effective feedback.

An implication of the need for feedback is that most practice should be public. Far too much practice is covert—the student silently reading notes, reciting passages, going through flash cards, or answering worksheet problems. Even silent reading is less effective than reading aloud, partly because if the student reads aloud she can get feedback from the teacher.[17] When students do basketball drills, everything they do is in plain view for all to see. This keeps them alert and active. Nobody ever fell asleep during basketball practice.

Practice sessions should be short and spaced. Anyone who has ever put off studying until the last minute (which is to say, everybody) knows that a long practice session may get a student through an exam, but it doesn't yield much in the way of long-term retention.

Research has consistently shown that several short practice sessions get better results than one long one. For instance, Harry Bahrick and Elizabeth Phelps had college students study 50 English–Spanish word equivalents in seven practice sessions. Some students had all seven sessions on the same day. Some had one session a day for seven consecutive days. And some had one session a month for seven months. Eight *years* after their final practice session the students took a test on what they had studied. The result was that students who practiced at 30-day intervals recalled about twice as much as those who studied once a day, and those who studied once a day recalled more than those who did all their studying in one day.[18]

It's not clear what the optimum interval between practice sessions is. Bahrick suggested one month, but C. Rovee-Collier found that two-day intervals worked well.[19] The ideal plan might be to begin with daily or more frequent practice sessions and gradually increase the intervals to one or two months.

Practice should continue beyond accuracy. Overlearning—continuing to practice even after you "know it"—is important to long-term retention.[20] The teacher's motto should be, "What is worth learning is worth over-learning."

Many experts from different theoretical perspectives (including educational researcher Benjamin Bloom, behavior analyst Ogden Lindsley, and cognitive psychologist John R. Anderson) believe that students should practice until they achieve *automaticity* or *fluency*.[21] (Automaticity is the term favored by cognitive psychologists and educational researchers, while behavior analysts prefer the term fluency. I will use the latter term, since it's less cumbersome.)

Fluency is defined as a performance that is accurate, smooth (i.e., done without hesitation), and relatively fast. A convenient and objective measure of fluency is number correct per minute, meaning the number of times a task is performed correctly in a one-minute timing. For example, if Russell reads a passage aloud for one minute and in that time reads 100 words with three mistakes, his fluency rate is 97 cpm (correct per minute). Similarly, if he multiplies three-digit numbers (such as 241 × 365) and solves three problems correctly in a minute, then his fluency is three cpm.

Fluency applies to high- as well as low-level skills. A student might, for example, read aloud in a foreign language at 150 cpm or solve algebraic word problems of a certain difficulty at three cpm.

One way to achieve fluency is through timed trials. For example, the student might read a passage as quickly as she can, recite as much of a poem as she can, identify the subject and verb of as many sentences as she can, or go through as many anatomy flash cards as she can in one minute. Typically the student records the number of correct performances during each trial. A variation of the procedure is to do a certain amount of work (read a passage with a certain number of words, for example) and record the time it took to accomplish the task.[22]

Some experts recommend introducing fluency training into practice at the very beginning of a learning unit. But I think most fluency excepts would recommend that teachers begin with more conventional practice, with its emphasis on accuracy, and then switch to fluency practice when the students' accuracy level is high.

Practice should be varied. Varying the materials used in practice, as well as the kind of practice, is important for best results. Variety helps maintain the sense of challenge, prevents boredom, and improves transfer.

Practice at reading is very important to the development of that skill, but that does not mean students have to read nothing but basal readers or textbooks. They can read Beatrix Potter, J. K. Rowling, R. L. Stine, or C. S. Lewis. They can read *Stone Soup, Seventeen,* or *Reader's Digest.* Giving students a say in what they read whenever possible makes practice more palatable, and probably more beneficial.

Variety in practice also improves transfer. For example, if a student is learning auto mechanic skills, he should practice on a variety of cars, and preferably in a variety of garages. Similarly, if students are to transfer skills at public speaking to the many situations they will face (as an officer of a civic club, group leader in a military unit, political party organizer, union representative, or organizer of a church fund-raising function), a monthly book report will not do the job. They need to practice speaking in a variety of settings—to a group of peers while working on a project, to a jury in a mock trial, to the judges in a debate, to team members in a competition.

We can never anticipate and duplicate all the different situations in which what we teach may need to be used, but the greater the variety of practice situations, the greater the transfer to new situations.

Practice should be fun. As noted, providing variety in practice helps prevent boredom, but practice should be more than not boring; most of the time it should be something students enjoy.[23] Those who dismiss all forms of practice as "drill and kill" assume that practice is inherently unpleasant. Any parent who has ever inserted earplugs to escape the irritation of hearing a child play *Jingle Bells* on the piano for the thirty-seventh time ("Oops! I messed up. Gotta do it again!"), knows that children often enjoy practicing.[24] In trying to make practice fun, don't forget to consult the experts at fun—the students themselves.

Some of the skills we want students to practice are things the students actually enjoy doing, and they do them so frequently that teachers make rules against doing them. For instance, students write notes to one another, talk and listen to their neighbors, read books and magazines, and work on crossword puzzles. Teachers often forbid these activities, not because they are bad but because they compete with other activities on which the teacher wants the students to focus. But it is sometimes possible to let students practice skills in ways that don't interrupt the lesson. A time might be set aside during which students can write and send notes to one another and to the teacher. Working in pairs or in small groups on assignments gives them an opportunity to practice oral language skills. Students who have completed an assignment can be allowed to read a magazine. Spelling and vocabulary words can be incorporated into crossword puzzles.[25]

It's true that these kinds of practice don't always provide the sort of feedback that students need to improve. Consider this hypothetical student note to a classmate: "Did you here what Hary did on the playground today he ate a betel Billy dared him. and he did it was really gross i mean really gorss it was a big betel." The recipient of such a missive is not likely to point out the numerous errors in punctuation, spelling, and grammar. But the errors will make deciphering the note challenging, which in itself may be useful to the recipient and may also give him an appreciation for the value of writing rules.

Kids like to sing, and the A-B-C song is a good way of practicing the alphabet. Singing *Old MacDonald Had a Farm* is a fun way of learning about the kinds of animals on farms. Rhyming poems, especially silly ones, are fun to learn, and some can provide practice in facts or skills as well as develop an appreciation for rhythm and imagery. Web blogs offer another form of practice in writing, as do letters to editors, government officials, authors, and the school principal.

All sorts of games can provide practice. Give students anagrams made up of vocabulary, spelling, science, or history terms. (e.g., Newton formulated the law of TYGAVRI; George Washington and his troops endured a very hard winter in YLAVLE RFGOE.)

Kids love to play games in which they race with peers to find things; why not have them race to find knowledge? You might, for example, turn a practice session on library skills into a scavenger hunt. Each item found (the ISBN of a certain book, the population of Belgium) might provide a clue to the location of a treasure, such as a free reading period, a congratulatory note to the children's parents, or the right to choose the next book for class reading. Pairs or small groups of students might compete to find the treasure. The same basic idea could be applied to practicing Web-browsing skills.

The spelling bee is a game that can be an effective form of practice, with some modification. Normally a student is ejected once she misspells a word, but that leaves her sitting on the sidelines; we can do better. Suppose that names on each team are chosen at random. A selected student attempts to spell a word, and then his name is put back into the bowl so he can be called on again. Or a student who misspells a word gets a second chance at spelling it correctly later on. If a student spells a word correctly on the first try, she receives two points; if she does so the second time, she gets one point. That way, students have a strong incentive to learn the words they miss.

Another game many teachers use is modeled after the TV game show, *Jeopardy*. Students pick a category and compete to answer a question in that category, winning points instead of bucks. I have used this game with college students as a way of reviewing material before tests. All seem to enjoy it, and most prefer it to the standard review. Of course, there are all sorts of computer games that provide practice at academic skills and knowledge.

Many elementary school students enjoy choral drills if the teacher does them with some animation and encourages students to respond enthusiastically. Sometimes a little humor helps as well. Other forms of drill can be made fun by introducing a competitive element.[26] Students can be taught to go through flash cards quickly and to count the number they get right in one minute. They can record this number each day and strive to reach a certain fluency goal. I encourage students to use flash cards, and I hold a flash card competition with the winner receiving a silly prize. Even college students enjoy the exercise.

I have gone to some length in this chapter to make the case for practice. No, I do *not* advocate that the entire school day be devoted to choral drill, worksheets, flash cards, or other forms of repetitive activities. But if you want your students to achieve a high level of mastery, to retain what they learn, and to be able to use what they learn in a variety of situations, *there is no way to achieve those goals without providing lots of practice.*

You will see the value of practice when you . . .

Assess Progress

> *What gets measured, gets done.*
> —Peter Drucker

Ask a parent or a teacher to define educational assessment and she will probably say something like "The evaluation of student progress." If you talk to her about what evaluation means, sooner or later she's likely to admit it means assigning grades. So the commonly accepted wisdom is that we assess student progress in order to assign grades.[1] It follows from this logic that assessment, which usually comes in the form of paper-and-pencil tests, marks the end of a period of instruction: the end of a lesson, end of a unit, end of a chapter, end of a term.

I suggest an entirely different approach to assessment. In this view, assessment means *gathering information from students to guide instruction.*[2] It is the process of finding out what you have succeeded in teaching, and what you have yet to teach.

It follows from this view that assessment marks the *beginning* of the instructional process, not the end. That may seem perverse, so let me explain. Let's imagine that your curriculum guide requires that you teach your third grade darlings that all things can be divided into one of three categories: animal, vegetable, or mineral. You give a lesson on this wisdom. Did your students "get it"? By way of review, you ask some questions:

YOU: What are the three categories into which all things fall? Jennifer?

JENNIFER: Animals, vejables, and minerals.

YOU: That would be *vegetables* but, yes, you're right. Very good. So, let's classify some objects. What is a cricket—animal, vegetable, or mineral? Don?

DON: Animal.

YOU: Right. How about an apple? Alberto?

ALBERTO: Ahhhh . . . vegetable?

YOU: Right.

JENNIFER: An apple's not a vejable; an apple's a fruit.

YOU: Well, yes, you're right, Jennifer, but it comes from a plant, so it's a kind of vegetable.

JENNIFER: Uh-uh. My mommy says fruits and vejables are different.

YOU: Well. . . .

RALPH: What about a flower? That's not an animal or a mineral, but it's not a vegetable either. You can't *eat* a flower. Well, I guess you *could* eat it, but it's not food. Is it?

YOU: Well. . . .

HEATHER: My brother ate a stone once. Does that mean a stone is a vegetable?

YOU: Well. . . .

DON: I don't get it.

Back to the drawing board, right? You have *covered* the material in the curriculum guide, but you apparently haven't *taught* it. As your assessment continues—for that is what you are doing under guise of review— you will determine the depth of your students' ignorance, but it is already clear that you have work to do.[3]

As you proceed, you will be thinking about how to get through to them. "Would it be better," you wonder, "if I used the term *plants,* and later brought in the term *vegetable* as a rough synonym? Maybe I could put some examples of animals on the board and ask them what they all have in common, then do the same with plants and minerals. Or maybe I should introduce the notion of putting things in the category they're in *or closest to,* acknowledging that the real world is sometimes not perfectly neat." In any case, you know you need to go at it again, perhaps in a different way.

If your assessment tells you that the students have not learned much, you will know what to teach. If your assessment persuades you that your students have learned well, then you are ready to move on to something new, and again you know what to teach. In either case, assessment marks the beginning of instruction, not the end.

Assessment is an ongoing process, intimately entwined with instruction. It is much more complicated than giving weekly quizzes and an end-of-term exam. There are two broad forms of assessment, informal and formal.

Informal assessment refers to the observations the teacher makes during the process of teaching. A teacher is doing informal assessment when he asks himself, "Does that wrinkled brow mean Johnny doesn't understand what I just said, or does it mean he has a stomachache?" He is doing assessment when he notices that several of his female students slam their notebooks on their desks and wonders, "Another bad day with the new gym teacher?" He is doing assessment when he notices his students always seem to get sleepy on rainy days, and thinks, "Maybe I need to brighten up the room a bit."

Assessment means gathering information from students that can help you teach. If a student is squinting because she needs glasses, that information can markedly improve instruction. The teacher might, for example, move the student closer to the chalkboard, provide a magnifying glass so she can read texts, and take steps to help her get fitted with glasses. Assessment means considering the level of understanding sug-gested by the questions students ask and the comments they make. The discovery and Socratic teaching methods (see chapter 3), though not very efficient instructionally, are very useful ways of both reviewing and assessing learning. Pair and group learning exercises also provide oppor-tunities for assessing performance.

Informal assessment includes noting the skill students show when participating in or viewing a debate, a discussion, or a skit. It means noticing whether a student makes eye contact with others while giving an oral report, which words he stumbles on when reading aloud, and whether he takes a moment to think before answering a difficult ques-tion. It also means watching a student's breathing pattern as he does the butterfly stroke, noting whether he gets up on his toes when he serves a tennis ball, and wandering around the room to monitor student progress on a workbook exercise.

Informal assessment relies a good deal on a host of nonverbal mes-sages—the frown that suggests confusion, the heavy sigh of frustration, the finger tapping of impatience, the gaping mouth and wide eyes of sur-prise, the smile of understanding. This sort of assessment on the fly is essential to the progress of a lesson.

Some teachers pay no heed. They "cover" the material, pushing on regardless of how their students react. These are the teachers who equate teaching with talking, who say, as so many teachers said to me when I was a student, "It is my job to present this material; it is your job to learn it."

These instructors are puzzled and annoyed when students straggle into class, drag their heels when asked to do something, complain about trivial issues, make excuses to leave the room, ask irrelevant questions, chat among themselves, get into mischief, and do poorly on tests. And these teachers typically see no connection between their failure to heed the signals students send and the rude, unruly group their class has become. "Students today," these teachers will say, "just don't want to learn."

The teacher's task is not to "present" or "cover" material; it is to help students learn. To reach that goal, the teacher must assess how well students are doing moment by moment. Students will let you know in a hundred different ways. Ignore these messages at your peril.

Important as informal assessment is to the progress of a lesson, it is not always a reliable measure of what students have learned. One of my college instructors illustrated this with a personal anecdote. He had a handsome, bright-looking student who sat in the front row. The student came to class every day, smiled at all the instructor's jokes, nodded his head at appropriate moments, and seemed to follow the lectures easily. But when the instructor gave the first exam, he was astonished to find that this student had learned practically nothing. The instructor's infor-mal assessment of the student's progress was totally false.

Of course, the instructor may not have done a good job of informally assessing the student's learning. Evidently, he did not ask this student any questions, nor elicit comments from him. But even the best teachers can be fooled by informal assessments. Sometimes the slovenly, surly looking boy with green hair slouched deeply in his chair at the back of the room and looking more asleep than awake is learning more than the kid sitting upright in the front row, wearing a jacket and tie, and taking notes furiously.

Even when the teacher's informal assessment is correct, it provides only limited information to guide instruction. Suppose you have 20 students in your class. You give a lesson on identifying the subject of a sentence. You define *subject,* give simple examples, and then gradually increase their complexity. During the lesson, you ask students to identify the subjects of several sentences. How many times can you call on Keesha during the course of the lesson? Once, twice, maybe three times? Even if you think you have an accurate idea of which students need more help, what help do they need? Unless your class has fewer than six students, informal assessment can't usually provide you with that kind of detail. For that, you must rely on formal assessment.

Formal assessment consists of using tools to gather data to determine what a student needs to learn. Most discussions of assessment have in mind formal assessment, and most focus on the use of paper-and-pencil tests.[4]

There are two basic kinds of test items, objective and subjective. Objective items are those for which the correct answers can be specified unambiguously. Common examples of objective items include multiple choice, fill in the blank, matching, sequencing, and true-false. Less familiar examples include crossword puzzles, anagrams, and what I call sentagrams (sentences with the words in scrambled order) and paragrams (paragraphs in scrambled order).

Some objective items measure the rate at which a student performs. For example, a student may go through flash cards one at a time. The number of correct responses in a one-minute session indicates the degree of fluency achieved.[5] Or students may be timed as they solve ten math problems of a particular type, as they recite the alphabet, or as they name the phyla of animals called out by the teacher (e.g., jellyfish—coelenterata).

Usually there is only one correct answer to an objective item, but this is not necessarily the case. Consider the question, "Name a means of motorized mass transportation that is typically faster than a bus." Correct answers include train, plane, and subway. There is more than one correct answer, but all the correct answers can be specified in advance. This means that there is an objective standard by which the test can be scored. In fact, the word *objective* refers to the lack of judgment required in scoring the test. Ask two people to score an objective test, and most of the time you will get exactly the same score from both. In fact, some objective items (most notably multiple choice) can be scored by machines.

Objective items are appealing because they can be scored quickly and usually generate few complaints from students. Their chief disadvantage is that it is more difficult to write objective items that get at more than simple recall. It can be done, however. Consider the following question, which is similar to those I confronted in a course on theories of counseling:

> A counselor meets a new client for a therapy session. The client begins by saying, "I guess I should start by telling you about my relationship with my mother. That's the way this is done, isn't it?" The therapist replies, "Therapy is new to you, so it must be difficult to know how to start." Of the following, the therapist's comment is most consistent with the therapeutic methods of:
>
> a. Sigmund Freud
>
> b. Carl Rogers
>
> c. Joseph Wolpe
>
> d. Albert Ellis

The hypothetical situation in the question was not presented in the course, so answering it was not a matter of simple recall. Instead, the test taker had to use what he knew about the various counseling theories to infer which approach the therapist had adopted. For example, given what you know about Freud, you can probably eliminate him fairly easily, since he *did* encourage clients to talk about their parents and would have been more likely to say something like, "Yes, that's a good place to start."[6]

Even college students may be taken aback by such questions. I recall one student complaining after the exam, "I studied my notes and the text very carefully and there was *no mention* of a client asking if he should start by talking about his mother!" He was right, of course, but he had missed the point. The task was not to *recall* the answer, but to *deduce* it from what he had learned about counseling theories.

Despite this evidence, you may still find it difficult to believe that some skills can be measured with objective items. You may be thinking, for example, "There is no way you can test a student's ability to punctuate a sentence or write a good essay with fill-in-the-blank or multiple choice questions." Well, maybe you can. Consider this item:

> In the following sentence, put a comma in each blank if required; if a comma is not required, leave the blank empty:
>
> Mr. Parker____ the principal___ of our school____ agreed to dye his hair____ green if everyone in the first grade _____ could recite the alphabet in less than 30 seconds___ by the end of the month.

Or, consider this item on paragraph organization:

> The numbered sentences in the following paragraph are out of order. Indicate the correct order of the sentences by writing the numbers here in the order in which they should appear: ___ ___ ___ ___.

(1) But he that stands it now, deserves the love and thanks of man and woman. (2) The summer soldier and the sunshine patriot will, in this crisis, shrink from the service of his country. (3) These are the times that try men's souls. (4) Tyranny, like hell, is not easily conquered.[7]

If the paragraph above is familiar to you, the item will be largely a measure of recall, but it is possible to use the approach with original material, in which case higher-level skills are measured. This item could also be presented as a multiple choice question with each alternative offering a different arrangement.

You can see that the commonly held view that objective items can measure only simple recall is clearly (a) false (b) true (c) sometimes true, sometimes false (d) irrelevant. (The correct answer is a.)

One problem with objective items, especially the multiple choice type, is that they can teach errors. A multiple choice item usually involves four or five choices, all but one of which are wrong. To be any good, some of these decoy answers must be plausible. Therefore, the student will sometimes select these credible but incorrect answers. Unfortunately, when students do this, they are likely to remember their answer as correct. In other words, the test teaches them misinformation.[8] Even when students are told later that the answer is wrong, the misinformation tends to stick. This is another example of the stubborn error effect discussed earlier.[9]

Another problem with objective test items is that, while students may not argue much about the answers, they do sometimes object to the wording of the question:

- "Number 9 was a trick question! It shouldn't be counted."
- "Just about everybody got number 13 wrong, so it must be a bad question. It should be thrown out."
- "In number 5, I thought you meant. . . ."

Fortunately for you, the merits of such complaints can be established scientifically with a simple procedure called item analysis. (Doing an item analysis does *not* mean, as so many teachers think, throwing out the items that most students got wrong. A bad item is one that students who don't know the subject are as likely to get right as students who do. See Appendix B.) You do the item analysis and, based on the results you get, eliminate bad items. Then you explain to students how the item analysis was done and which items were eliminated. (Though I have not done this with elementary grade students, I suspect that average fifth graders will be able to follow the logic.) *Then* you return the students' tests and discuss all the items, including those that were thrown out. This procedure pretty much eliminates complaints.

Subjective test items are those for which several different answers are acceptable. "What was George Washington's most important achievement?" is such a question. If a subjective test is scored by two different people, they will likely come up with two different scores.

Suppose a student writes, in answer to the previous question, "After the revolution, George Washington was immensely popular and could have become king of America, thus making America a monarchy. His greatest achievement was that he declined to do this." Some people might consider this a very weak answer. What about keeping the troops together through the long winter at Valley Forge? What about guiding the country through its first eight years as a nation? Others might think the answer very insightful. With subjective items, the judgment of the instructor is very important in assessing the answers.

One advantage of subjective items is that it is fairly easy to write questions measuring understanding and application. The chief problem with subjective items is that they are difficult to score. They typically take a good deal of time and are likely to generate complaints from students and even parents. Some students will argue with you forever about George Washington's greatest achievement. And there is no practical way of doing an item analysis of subjective items.

"Is this test to find out what I know, or to find out what I don't know?"

George B. Abbott

Which is better, objective or subjective items? For teacher-made tests, the best idea may be to use several kinds of items, both objective and subjective, or use objective items one day and subjective items on another.

Although testing is a complicated topic, there are some rules of thumb you can follow to increase the usefulness of your tests.

The best reason for giving a test is to find out what you need to teach. Tests are widely used to assign grades, but testing ought to be mainly about discovering what the teacher needs to teach. In time, you will forget that. You will get wrapped up, as all teachers do, in the use of tests to determine grades. When this happens, I hope that you will get the feeling that you are forgetting something, and—after a struggle—recall that the real purpose of testing is to determine what to teach next. Everything else I can say about testing derives from this understanding of its purpose.

Tests should be short and given frequently. They should be short to minimize the time taken away from instruction. If you have studied test construction, my suggestion may surprise you. It is a given in the field of test construction that short tests have less validity than longer ones. When you are talking about standardized tests, such as the *Iowa Tests of Basic Skills*, this rule of thumb is important. But standardized tests are usually given once a year and cover a great deal of information. Teacher-made tests, when given frequently, are intended to show only what students have learned from one or two lessons. It doesn't take an hour-long test to do that.

Tests should be frequent because the longer you teach in the dark, the less you will see. You need feedback about what students have learned in order to know what to teach next. The more you teach without that knowledge, the greater the risk that some students are falling behind and the more difficult it will be to help them catch up.

Frequent, short tests, such as daily quizzes, have other advantages over infrequent longer assessments, such as exams. Frequent testing results in a steadier rate of studying, so students learn and retain more.[10] The shorter a test is, the lower the risk of humiliation to the student, so the less anxiety the test is likely to create. The less anxiety, the more pleasant school becomes.

Frequent short tests are also preferable when it comes to assigning grades. The teacher who gives only two exams in a marking period is likely to hear many excuses from students. "Everything I know seems to emigrate to Canada when I'm faced with a big exam." "I had a bad hair day." "I was worried about my great aunt Ethel, who thought she might need an operation for an ingrown toenail." "That was the week I had the flu. The whole time I took the exam, I was concentrating on keeping my breakfast down." Frequent, short tests will sharply reduce complaints and excuses. It's hard for a student to point to a string of daily quizzes and say with a straight face, "I was sick all those days."

A test should be a learning experience.[11] Pair and group quizzes, in which students share what they know with others in an attempt to answer quiz questions, reduce the stress of tests and may help students learn about a subject. Students can also learn when the quiz is put in the form of a puzzle or game. I have used crossword puzzles this way. Students can often deduce the answer to one question by filling in answers from other answers and using the clues it provides. There are inexpensive software programs, such as Crossword Magic® and Wordsearch Creator,® designed to help you create puzzles that you can use as either quizzes or exercises.

Whenever possible, provide immediate and specific feedback. For students to learn from a test, they must receive specific feedback about their performance. This does not mean merely telling the student his score. Saying to a student, "You answered eight out of the 10 items correctly," may reduce his anxiety, but it does nothing to improve his mastery of the subject. It is essential to go over each item on a quiz or test. Nor is even this sort of feedback sufficient. Students get more from reviewing a test if the class discusses *why* each answer is correct and other answers are incorrect. It is best to provide this feedback immediately after the test. Remember that when students take a test, they may be learning incorrect information. The longer the delay between answering a question and learning the correct answer, the more difficult it will be for the student to "unlearn" errors. Specific feedback delivered immediately after a test is probably the best way to forestall the stubborn error effect.

Test on what you want students to be able to do. Teachers *say* they want students to understand and be able to apply information, not just to parrot facts. But if they do not test for understanding and application, the message to students is that what counts is recalling facts.

Tests should be cumulative. They should include some items covered earlier in the course. Teachers *say* they don't want students to learn things just for a test and then forget about them, yet once they have completed a unit, many teachers never ask questions on that topic again. If you include items on old material, students will review old material throughout the year, and not just prior to the final exam.

What you test shows what you value. Many teachers seldom include test items on presentations made by students or guests (such as parents), or on comments made by students in class discussions. Some teachers ask no questions about things seen or heard on field trips or on videos or films seen in class. Teachers *say* that all of these things are important, and they *say* that students can learn from many sources, including one another. But when students take a test, what do they find? Typically, only questions on material covered by the teacher or in a text. Why should students take an interest in these other things when your tests say they aren't important?

Make tests, not the teacher, the enemy. Tests are usually important in determining grades, and grades are important in obtaining parental approval and in achieving academic and career goals. Because of this, students are naturally inclined to see the teacher's tests, and therefore the teacher, as their opponent. Teacher-made tests help create an adversarial relationship between teachers and students.

Jaime Escalante, the high school math teacher made famous by the film, *Stand and Deliver,* avoided this problem by making the Advanced Placement tests in math the enemy. The in-class quizzes were, as far as the students were concerned, merely a way of measuring their progress in preparing for the AP. In essence, Escalante said to his students, "You and I must work together very hard to defeat our common enemy, the AP test." Escalante's students saw him not as their opponent, but as their partner. He was like a coach preparing his team for the big game. Not all teachers can use AP tests in this way, but they can make their own tests the adversaries they are determined to help students defeat.

One of the things contributing to the feeling that students and teachers are on opposite sides is the fact that some students will cheat. The best way to deal with cheating is to prevent it as much as possible. Cheating is less likely to occur if you make it clear before the very first test that you take cheating very seriously, and if you specify what the consequences for cheating will be. Many teachers never do this, which gives students the impression that cheating "is no big deal." Let them know that in your class, it *is* a big deal.

Giving frequent, short tests, and not basing grades solely on tests, reduces the incentive to cheat. Remaining attentive during tests will also discourage those tempted to use crib sheets or spy on a neighbor's paper. If these efforts don't work, you can have students spread out, space permitting, or you can separate those who tend to share answers.

Preventing cheating is far more desirable than catching and punishing cheaters, since the latter tends to put you and your students into adversarial roles. Assessment is something teachers ought to do to help students learn. If few students see assessment that way, then it is our fault as teachers.

The big thing to remember about assessment is that its purpose is to inform instruction. But assessment is an evaluation of the *teacher's* progress as much as the student's. The inescapable fact is that every time your students fail to learn, you have failed to teach. The harsh reality is that assessment isn't so much about identifying your students' failures as it is your own.

If your assessment shows that you have been successful, chances are you will be able to . . .

Motivate Successfully

> *Nothing succeeds like success.*
>   —French saying

Periodically I am invited to talk to the students of a high school psychology class. On one occasion, the teacher told me the students were very enthusiastic about psychology, had a lot of questions for me, and were looking forward to my visit with great excitement.

I arrived just before the start of class and watched the students take their seats. As I began talking to them, I discovered that, contrary to what the teacher had told me, the students were not expecting me, had no questions they were burning to ask, and had no discernible interest in psychology. In fact, three weeks into the semester they could neither define nor spell the word *psychology*.[1]

As I looked about the room, I saw an all-too-familiar scene: Two boys sitting side by side rested their heads on their desks and feigned sleep. Other students slumped in their seats in nearly horizontal positions. A typical student sat hunched over her desk, her head supported by a hand that was, in turn, held in place by an elbow propped against the desk. She looked like a porch under repair. I asked her casually what she intended to do after high school. "Gotuhcollege," was her one-word reply. And what do you want to study in college? She answered with a desultory shrug. Well, then, I persisted, why go to college? "Gettuhgoodjob."

All in all, it was a depressing sight: A group of young people who looked for all the world like patients in a nursing home: bored, tired of life, waiting for the end. The class was a psychology class in name only. In reality it was one of those human catch basins to which slackers are shunted so that they won't contaminate other students.

Why are some students eager to learn, while others could care less? The dominant theory is that the slackers lack motivation. These amotivated students, as they are called, are believed to have a basic defect that lies somewhere within themselves. The exact source and location of this defect is never specified. Is the brain sluggish? Is there a hormone deficiency? A need for vitamins? Those who blame the students for lacking motivation seldom ask, let alone answer, these questions. It is enough for them to say, "It's pointless to try to teach Charles. He has no motivation." Others agree. "Give me students who are motivated," they say, "and I'll teach them. But if students don't want to learn, I can't teach them."[2]

There are serious problems with this view of motivation. Go into any kindergarten class in September and you will see very few amotivated students. Even students who come from homes where education is not valued are typically excited to be in kindergarten and are eager to learn. If

motivation is something inside the child, then it is clearly present in virtually all students at age five. So why is it that by the end of third grade
many kids no longer care about learning anything in school? Does motivation evaporate like water? Do some students have a small store of
motivation that they use up in a few years, like a car that runs out of gas?
And if students who don't care to learn lack motivation, why are they not
amotivational in the gym, or in the garage where they tinker with cars?
Why are so many amotivated students hard working and ambitious in
their after-school jobs? The internal theory of motivation, though widely
accepted by teachers and the public at large, simply will not do.

The alternative theory is that motivation isn't something inside the
student, like some miniature Tolkien beast, but a reasonable reaction of
the student to her experience. The good thing about this view is that it
puts motivation in the student's surroundings, literally within the
teacher's grasp.[3]

Consider who the amotivated students are. For the most part, they
are the students who read too slowly to get to the end of a story in the
time allotted. They are the students who have not mastered short division but are asked to follow a lesson on long division. They are the students who cannot write a clear sentence but are asked to write a story.
The amotivated students are, in short, the ones who have had a steady
diet of failure, disappointment, frustration, and humiliation in connection with school learning.[4] They are the ones who find the grapes are
almost always out of reach, and who conclude, like Aesop's fox, that they
are not worth eating.

To most teachers, not trying to learn is irrational. "If you don't learn,"
they tell the student, "you will have no future. You won't be able to get a
job. You'll be a bum or a criminal. Is that what you want?" But when you
realize that motivation is not inside the student, but in his immediate
surroundings, his lack of interest in school learning is perfectly rational.
What is irrational is for a student to beat his head against a wall day after
day without success. And success is what motivation is all about.

The internal view of motivation assumes that motivation is the key
to success, but in fact success is the key to motivation. Put another way,
students are not successful because they are motivated; they are motivated because
they have been successful. If teachers want to motivate students, they must
see to it that they are often successful.[5]

Success means achieving something—mastering a skill, solving a
problem, discovering a fact, or creating something pleasing to the senses.
This book can be viewed as a discussion of how to make such successes
possible. The implicit assumption behind this effort is that everyone
enjoys success, and that success creates a desire for new challenges and
new successes.

I think the assumption is valid, but the satisfaction that comes from
success at a task is not always sufficient. One student may take delight in

correctly diagramming a sentence and be eager to do more, while another equally capable student may not. Students who have a long history of failure are particularly reluctant to attempt the challenges a teacher provides, since to do so is to risk further humiliation and frustration. They must be coaxed into success.

There are times, then, when success may mean earning the praise of a teacher, the admiration of other students, or receiving symbols of success, such as gold stars, certificates, awards, privileges (taking the roll, reading out the new spelling words), and even small prizes.

As soon as someone mentions the idea of providing gold stars and the like, or even praise, many people object.[6] The belief is widespread in education that such "extrinsic" rewards actually undermine interest in learning.[7] Everyone interested in motivating students will probably agree that if rewards reduce interest in the rewarded activity, then they are counterproductive and ought to be banished from the classroom. In some schools, they already have been banished.[8] When I suggested in the pages of *Phi Delta Kappan* that there was a place for rewards in the classroom, an

"We think your hobby is gardening, Miss Finch, because you're always planting in us the seeds of success."

George B. Abbott

elementary school principal wrote to express his disapproval. Every fall, he said, he pulls his new teachers aside and warns them never to praise student achievements because that would take away their motivation.[9]

So widespread is the belief that rewards are bad (in education it has become one of those things that "everyone knows") that I must explain why I think that what "everyone knows" is wrong.[10]

Mark Lepper and his colleagues conducted one of the first studies suggesting that rewards undermine interest.[11] The researchers began by observing nursery school children in their classroom as they played with a variety of toys. Some of the children showed a particularly strong interest in drawing with felt-tip pens. These children became the focus of the study.

Two weeks later the researchers returned to the school and took each of the study children, one at a time, to another room where they could draw with felt-tip pens. The researchers assigned each child to one of three groups: expected reward, unexpected reward, and no reward. The researchers told children in the expected-reward group that they would receive a "Good Player Award" if they drew some pictures. The researchers gave children in the unexpected-reward group the same award but did not mention it in advance. Children in the no-reward group neither received nor heard about an award.

One week later, the researchers returned to the classroom to observe the children as they played with various toys and recorded how much time each of the study children spent drawing. They discovered that the children in the promised-reward group spent less time drawing than they had before being rewarded. Those who received the same reward unexpectedly, and those who received no reward, showed no change in the amount of interest in drawing. Thus, an expected reward (but not an unexpected one) reduced interest in the rewarded activity.[12]

The Lepper study is fairly typical of the experiments done over the past 35 years on the effects of rewards on interest in a rewarded activity. Many of these studies show a detrimental effect from rewards. The findings are counterintuitive, so they have been widely reported. Education writer Alfie Kohn, who is surely the harshest critic of rewards, has probably done more than anyone to promote the idea that rewards are bad. In his book, *Punished by Rewards: The Trouble with Gold Stars, Incentive Plans, A's, Praise, and Other Bribes*, he writes, "One study after another has demonstrated that the more someone is rewarded for doing something (or doing something well), the less interest that person is likely to have in whatever he or she was rewarded for doing."[13]

Pretty devastating stuff, huh? It is little wonder that so many educators have embraced the idea that rewards of all shapes and sizes are bad. But this is not merely a topic for debate at academic roundtables. It is an issue with profound implications for what teachers do in classrooms. Are teachers who give gold stars to students guilty of educational malpractice? Is the principal who tells teachers not to praise students right to do so? Are rewards really so bad that they should be banished from the classroom?

No, they are not. That is not merely my opinion. It is, I believe, the opinion of every researcher who has studied the effects of rewards, including Mark Lepper, David Greene, Edward Deci, Teresa Amabile, and others who have found negative effects. So far as I know, no one who has done research on the motivational effects of reward has ever concluded that teachers should never provide them. No educational researcher, no social psychologist, no cognitive psychologist, no behavior analyst.[14] *Not one.* And with good reason.

For one thing, if rewards are demotivating, why is it that we don't reward *undesirable* behavior? For example, people become overweight at least partly because they overeat. Why not pay them to eat? I know the idea sounds silly, but if rewards really are demotivating, then rewarding people for eating should make them lose interest in eating and the pounds should melt away. Or, how about this: Give tokens to alcoholics each time they down a bottle of Rot Gut. This will undermine their interest in alcohol, and they'll soon be teetotalers. Muggings are no problem, either: Every time a street thug mugs someone, track him down and give him a certificate. When he earns a hundred certificates, send him to Disneyland! If rewards are demotivating, he'll stop robbing people long before he gets on the bus.

Now, I know this is freakish thinking, but stay with me. If you really, really believe that the more someone is rewarded for doing something, the less interest that person will have in that activity, then it logically follows that people who engage in undesirable behavior, such as overeating, over-drinking, and mugging people, ought to be rewarded for that behavior. That way they will do it less often. Yet, so far as I know, no one has ever suggested rewarding undesirable behavior as a way of reducing its frequency. Not even Alfie Kohn, and certainly not any researcher. Why ever not? Could it be that no one really believes that rewards undermine motivation?

Here's another dilemma for the anti-reward argument: Why don't high school kids on the football team hate playing football? In fact, why does anyone stay on the football team? As Herb Childress points out, high school football players are bombarded with rewards. He writes:

> Football players get extraordinary amounts of approval: awards and banquets, letter jackets, banners around campus, school festivals, team photos, whole sections of the yearbook, newspaper coverage, trophies, regional and even state recognition for being the best. The whole community comes out to see them. We put them on floats and have parades. That doesn't happen for members of the consumer math class.[15]

If rewards are bad for students, coaches should have to drag students onto the field. Tardiness, absenteeism, and attrition ought to be major problems. If extrinsic rewards are demotivating, the philosophy club should have the largest membership of any group in school and the most enthusiastic members. They gather together to discuss the intricacies of Hegel and Kant, unencumbered by team jackets, cheering crowds, and other demoralizing rewards. So how come you didn't even know your high school *had* a philosophy club?

And then there's Alfie Kohn. Yes, Alfie Kohn, dedicated critic of all forms of reward. Mr. Kohn has given dozens, perhaps hundreds, of interviews and lectures on the dangers of rewards. Now, if public attention, praise, applause, speaking fees, and book royalties are rewards (and according to Mr. Kohn they certainly are), then Mr. Kohn should have lost all interest in criticizing rewards long, long ago. Yet despite all the rewards he has received for talking about the evils of reward, he is still talking about the evils of reward. He goes on and on like the Energizer Bunny.® Mr. Kohn himself is living proof that rewards need not undermine motivation.

But what about the Lepper study and other experiments that found that rewards undermine interest? Are they to be dismissed? No, definitely not. But neither are the many experiments that *don't* show detrimental effects.

For example, Ross Vasta and Louise Stirpe used gold stars to reward math work in third and fourth grade students who enjoyed math. Their experiment followed the format of the experiment of Lepper and colleagues. Each day for ten days, they observed the children during twenty-minute sessions when they could work as they pleased on three different kinds of math problems. The researchers recorded the amount of time each child spent on each kind of problem in order to determine each child's preference. Then, each day for seven days, every time a child completed three pages of his or her favorite kind of math problems, the researchers put a gold star next to the child's name on a chart.[16]

Notice that this study roughly parallels the experiment by Lepper and colleagues described earlier: There was a no-reward period, a reward period, and then another no-reward period. During the reward period, students received a tangible reward for engaging in an activity in which they had shown a strong interest. And finally, the researchers compared time spent on the rewarded activity before and after rewards to determine the effect of rewards on interest in the rewarded activity.

The results, however, were quite different from those the Lepper study obtained. This time the students spent as much time or more on their favorite activity *after* rewards as they had *before*. Nor was there any change in the amount or quality of work that the students did. There was, in other words, no evidence that rewarding an activity undermines interest in that activity.

Contrary to what "everybody knows," many other experiments have also found evidence that sensibly used rewards have no adverse effects on interest. As T. C. Mawhinney put it, undermining motivation with extrinsic rewards is "easier said than done."[17]

Rewards have proved especially useful in energizing amotivated students. For instance, adolescents and young adults in Louisiana received $3.40 an hour to participate in a summer program offering remedial instruction in reading and math and in job skills.[18] These young people were high-risk, low-income students whose academic skills were well below grade level. Many had a history of truancy and misbehavior. Yet the average gains in reading ability for those who completed the eight-week program was 1.2 grade levels. The average gain in math was 1.5 grade levels. These students advanced more in eight weeks than average students advance in an entire school year.[19]

I doubt if anyone involved with this program would say that the money rewards *produced* the gains in achievement. The hard work of the students and the teachers did that. But the rewards got the students to enter and stay in the program, and without that there would have been no gains.

But, the reward bashers might ask, what happened after the program ended? Were the students in this program less interested in reading and math than they had been before they got paid for studying? There are no data on this point, but a decline in academic interest seems unlikely since these students showed little interest in academics *before* the program. As Greene and Lepper point out, if students show no interest in school in the first place, it is silly to worry about rewards undermining interest. "Clearly," they write, "if a child begins with no intrinsic interest in an activity, there will be no intrinsic motivation to lose."[20]

Moreover, there is good reason to believe that rewards can *increase* interest in a rewarded activity. Yes, I said rewards can *increase* interest in a rewarded activity. The Vasta and Stirpe study described earlier illustrates this: Two weeks after the rewards ended, the children showed an *increased* interest in the rewarded activity.[21]

Reward researchers have long acknowledged that praise can increase interest in an activity. Edward Deci writes, for example,

> We found, for instance, that if we rewarded a student for each correct solution with statements such as "good, that's very fast for that one," his intrinsic motivation *increased* markedly. The 48 students told us that they liked the puzzle more, and spent more free time working on it, than the 48 students whom we had not so praised.[22]

Praise is not the only reward that can increase interest. It is said that the Greek mathematician Pythagoras had a desultory student. One day Pythagoras told the student he would pay him a certain sum for each new theorem he learned. The stratagem worked: The student learned theorems quickly, and he began to enjoy his work. Then one day Pythagoras said, "It is not profitable for me to pay you to learn theorems, so I won't teach you any longer." The student implored Pythagoras to continue, and offered to pay *him* for each new theorem he taught the student. Pythagoras agreed and soon recovered his money.

The story is probably apocryphal, but there is good evidence that tangible rewards can indeed increase intrinsic interest. The prominent social psychologist Albert Bandura argues, in fact, that extrinsic rewards are essential to the development of interests. He writes:

> Most of the things people enjoy doing for their own sake had little or no interest for them originally. Children are not born innately interested in singing operatic arias, playing tubas, solving mathematical equations, writing sonnets, or propelling shot-put balls through the air. . . . Positive incentives are often used to promote such changes.[23]

One of Kohn's favorite targets is the BookIt! program sponsored by Pizza Hut. In this program, each time a student reads a certain number of books, her teacher gives her a coupon she can redeem for a small pizza or some other prize. In the 2004–05 school year, some 22 million youngsters were involved in the program.

Kohn often tells people that education professor John Nicholls said the BookIt! program would likely produce "a lot of fat kids who don't like to read."[24] Neither Mr. Kohn nor Mr. Nicholls offers any evidence that BookIt! ever made *any* student fat or ever made *any* student dislike reading. In fact, neither offers any evidence that the program has had any adverse effects. However, there *is* evidence that the program produces solid benefits.

A survey conducted by an affiliate of the University of Rhode Island found that over 90% of teachers said the program had improved student reading ability.[25] Perhaps more importantly, 88% said that students in the program showed an *increased* interest in reading, and 89% said their students more often read for pleasure—surely a sign of increased interest. But since Pizza Hut sponsored the survey, let's not put too much faith in it.

Stephen and David Flora, who have no connection to Pizza Hut or the BookIt! program, surveyed college students who had participated in the BookIt! program as youngsters.[26] Most students had fond memories of the program, and about half thought that their reading skills improved as a result of it. Almost all (92%) said that BookIt! either had no effect on their enjoyment of reading or increased it.[27]

As you can see, the results of research on the demotivating effects of reward are mixed. Some evidence says that rewards can undermine interest, while other evidence says that they can increase interest. Which body of evidence is correct? The answer is: *both*. The lesson to be learned from the research evidence is that whether rewards are helpful or not depends on *how they are used*. I think all reward researchers are in agreement with this conclusion.

The implication is that teachers must learn to use rewards effectively. They must not abandon rewards but must become experts in their use. In the hope of encouraging you to do just that, I offer here a set of eight guidelines with which I believe most experts on rewards will agree:

First, provide rewards mostly when interest is low. In most of the studies that get negative effects, rewards are offered for things the student already enjoys doing. The Lepper study described earlier is typical. The researchers selected students who showed a particularly strong liking for drawing and then rewarded the students for drawing. But there is little reason to provide rewards for engaging in behavior that students already find intrinsically rewarding. The lesson is: When students enjoy doing something, offering rewards is not necessary and may not help. It's when interest in an activity is low that rewards are most beneficial.

When students are struggling to learn the alphabet, the multiplication table, or French verb conjugations, rewards can help keep them motivated. As skills advance, the rewards of the activity begin to come into play, and extrinsic rewards are not so important. "At first," says Stephen Flora, who did the survey of former BookIt! students, "a kid might read to get the pizza. Later they'll read to find out who done it, or who got the girl."[28]

Second, emphasize intangible rewards. Most studies that get negative effects use tangible rewards—things you can touch, such as candy, toys, jewelry, hats, pencils, and the Good Player Award used by Lepper. Tangible rewards are also more likely to cause other problems, such as distracting students from the assigned task.

Intangible rewards include praise, applause, hugs, winks, smiles, and the proverbial pat on the back. Intangible rewards, especially earned praise, are likely to *increase* interest in the rewarded activity.[29]

The approval of a teacher should be a powerful reward. If it isn't—if your students don't care whether you are pleased by their achievements—then something is seriously wrong. Your students should know that you are a caring person and that you want them to ace the test, answer the question correctly, and give a great oral report. Show that you are pleased at their successes. Often it will mean more to them than gold.

Third, when using tangible rewards, use the weakest reward that will motivate. The more desirable a tangible reward is, the more likely it is to cause problems. Small tangible rewards can, however, be put to good use.

I have used tangible rewards, mostly trivial prizes, to good effect in academic competitions during reviews and practice sessions. I may describe a prize as an item that will help the winner find his or her way in life. After the competition, the class discovers that the winner has won a cheap compass. Or the prize may be "a solar-powered clock," which turns out to be a small sundial I've made out of cardboard and tape. Discovering the nature of the joke is as much a prize as the item itself. Even adults enjoy this kind of thing, and it makes routine activities, such as practice and reviewing, more fun.[30]

If you work with disgruntled, underachieving adolescents with a history of absenteeism and disruptive behavior, you may have to offer a chance to win a more substantial prize, such as an inexpensive portable radio. (These are now available for about $5.) You might provide chits (specially marked bits of paper) that are thrown into a jar. The more the student learns, the more chits she receives, and the more chits, the better her chances of winning the radio. But generally, the student's happiness at earning the prize, whatever it is, will reflect pride at having mastered the task as much as for having won the prize.

Fourth, use rewards as surprises more often than as incentives. Most studies that get negative results offer rewards as an incentive for doing something. Once again the Lepper study is typical. The researchers promised some students a reward if they would draw pictures, and these students later showed less interest in drawing. But remember that the same reward had no adverse effects when it came as a surprise.[31] Unexpected rewards do not undermine interest.

Before rejecting all incentive programs, however, keep in mind that many carefully planned, long-term incentive programs (such as BookIt!) have gotten excellent results without reducing interest in the rewarded activity. Eugene Lang's I Have a Dream Foundation and Ewing Kauffman's Project Choice, both of which pay college expenses for at-risk youths who stay out of trouble and graduate from high school, have produced clear benefits.[32] Such programs may be especially helpful with disadvantaged students. A blue-ribbon panel on the characteristics that identify successful schools with a high proportion of poor and minority students found that one feature was "the use of motivating management systems (i.e., some form of contingent reward)."[33]

Fifth, give rewards when they have been earned. In most studies that show a decline in interest, the rewards are given without regard to the quality of the work done. Lepper's students, for example, merely had to draw for a given period. They could have scribbled like chimpanzees and still received the award. If, however, rewards reflect an achievement or real progress toward a goal, then interest in the activity usually increases.[34] As social psychologist Robert Eisenberger notes, "When you reward a child for high-quality work, you send a message that they're doing a good job. The reward motivates the child to keep trying and to take pride in their work."[35]

The importance of earning rewards applies to intangible as well as tangible rewards. Some teachers have gotten the silly idea that praise should be freely available, like peanuts at a cocktail party. But praise has little motivating power if it is not earned, and you cannot consistently fool children into believing they have earned praise when they have not.[36]

The standards for earning rewards, however, may vary widely from one student to another. A student with a long history of school failure might be rewarded for a genuine, even if unsuccessful, effort. If a student never participates in class discussion and one day timidly offers a comment, even a weak one, an approving smile and thank-you from the teacher may help her gain the courage to comment again.

Some teachers will no doubt object to the idea of requiring less from some students. "What is the teacher supposed to do," they may ask, "when George turns in a spelling paper with 20 words, and 19 of them are spelled incorrectly? Is the teacher really to say, 'Great. You got one right.'?" In fact, this may be exactly what the teacher should do. If George usually gets 20 out of 20 spelling words wrong or doesn't even attempt the test, then getting one right is progress.

Please don't misunderstand me. I am not suggesting that standards don't matter. What I am suggesting is that the most fundamental standard is progress. When students make progress, that progress should be recognized. The student who is praised today for getting one spelling word right may next week get two spelling words correct, and the week after that perhaps four correct. It is *progress* that should be recognized, even more than stellar performance, because progress can *lead* to stellar performance.

Sixth, identify the behavior being rewarded. It's important to let students know exactly what they did to earn a reward.[37] The focus should be on the student's behavior, not on some personal characteristic. In fact, rewarding personal traits can backfire. For example, Claudia Mueller and Carol Dweck praised fifth grade students on completing a math problem.[38] The researchers praised some students for being smart and praised others for working hard. Later they gave the students more difficult problems to work on. The kind of praise the students received affected how hard they worked on the new problems. The students who had been praised for being smart soon gave up on the new problems; those who had been praised for hard work persevered.

Mueller and Dweck hypothesize that praising for intelligence implies that if you have difficulty with a problem, you are not smart enough to do it and may as well quit. Praising for hard work implies that if you have difficulty with a problem, you just need to keep working.

Seventh, vary the reward to fit the student. Where rewards are concerned, one size does not fit all. For many students in many situations, clear evidence of progress is the only reward required to maintain motivation. For other students, the approval of the teacher may do the trick. For still others, a phone call to a parent praising the student's progress will work better. For some, a tangible reward such as a certificate may be necessary. It is part of the teacher's job to figure out what sort of rewards work best with each student.

Vladimir Nazlymov, a former Soviet Army Colonel turned fencing coach at Ohio State University, says, "If you are a bear, you like honey, like blueberry. If you are a tiger, you want meat. If you are tiger and I give you blueberry, it's no good. It's my job to see what you need and give it."[39]

Eighth, point out the natural rewards. B. F. Skinner urged teachers to shift student attention from rewards provided by the teacher to the "natural" rewards provided by the activity itself. The teacher, he observed, is not always going to be around to provide praise or a pat on the back.[40] You can, for instance, point to the fun to be had from humor and word play in poetry, or the pleasure in reading aloud with a friend. You can teach students that art is an opportunity to enjoy imagining oneself in a bucolic landscape or a fantasy world, or in a historical role. You can point to the fun they may get from impressing their parents with their knowledge. For most children it's a treat to watch Dad's eyes pop when the child uses a grown-up word such as *abate*, or see Mom's jaw drop as they explain how a difference in air pressure above and below an airplane's wings lifts the plane off the ground.

Learning can lead to other pleasures outside the classroom. The student who learns about bacterial cultures in school may be delighted to know that he can gather water samples from different sources (kitchen sinks, mud puddles, streams or ponds) and make his own cultures to bring to school for examination.

I hope these guidelines will help you use rewards effectively. But while I have tried to challenge the widespread view that rewards are bad, my aim is not to get you to offer lots of rewards. Rather, it is to get you to do whatever you must to help a student succeed. Rewards are merely one tool for doing that.

One way or another, the teacher's job is to move students along, to see to it that they get to the next rung on the ladder. If the teacher can do that, students' motivation will increase. In fact, as I said earlier, the most important thing to remember about motivation is this:

> *People are not successful because they are motivated;*
> *they are motivated because they have been successful.*

Teach so that your students have a lot of success, and you will have the most motivated students in school.

One way to help your students succeed is to . . .

Teach the Tools

> *Give us the tools, and we will finish the job.*
> —Winston Churchill (to President Roosevelt), 1941

One of my instructors at what was then Colorado State College was a frail-looking, elderly, straight-backed gentleman named Howard Blanchard. One day Dr. Blanchard, who always dressed like a banker, went to the chalkboard and drew a graph on the board with a line rising steadily from left to right. "This," he said, "represents the average growth of academic progress of the faster-learning students in a year of school."

He then drew another line, starting from nearly the same point but rising more slowly, so that the two lines grew further apart. "And this line," he went on, "represents the average growth of achievement of the slower-learning students over the course of the same year." The graph showed clearly that the slower students get further behind with each month. Dr. Blanchard noted that this pattern is repeated every year, so that by the end of the twelfth grade there is a huge gap in achievement between the two groups of students.

"Narrowing this achievement gap," he said, "is one of the major problems in education today." Forty years later, it still is.

The fact that some students learn a great deal more than others over the course of their education may seem perfectly natural, even inevitable. But why does it happen? And is it truly inevitable?

The most widely accepted answer to the *why* question is brainpower. Some students, it is argued, have better brains than others, either because of heredity or home environment. It is certainly well established that both heredity and home environment affect intelligence as measured by IQ tests and school success. But is the difference in learning rate due solely to differences in brains? There is good reason to believe there's more to it than that.

There is ample evidence that faster and slower learners behave differently when attempting to learn. For example, John Belmont and Earl Butterfield asked children to learn a series of letters.[1] They found that those with normal IQs paused regularly to repeat the preceding letters, while those with low IQs did not. As expected, the brighter students did better. But was it because they had better brains, or because of differences in how they approached the task? Belmont and Butterfield induced the youngsters with lower IQs to pause and repeat letters and found that they then did almost as well as the children with higher IQs. Most of the difference in learning was due not to differences in brain power, but rather to differences in how the kids tackled the task.

Repeating things to prevent forgetting is just one example of the many things that students can do to help themselves learn. Students who know about these tools and use them regularly learn more rapidly than students who don't. The faster learners are like workers digging a trench with a backhoe, while the slower learners are doing the job with a pick and shovel.

Does this mean that there are, after all, no differences among students in innate ability, that all students have exactly the same potential for learning? No, I don't think it does. But I think it does mean that one reason some students learn so much more than others is that they have learned *how* to learn. Mastering the tools of learning amplifies whatever ability a student has.

An implication of this *amplifier effect*, as I like to call it, is that if we teach *all* students the tools of learning, *all* students will learn more. However, the students who will benefit most will be those who are not already acquiring learning tools on their own or from their families. This means the learning gap Howard Blanchard talked about should diminish.[2]

Teachers cannot alter students' genes, they cannot usually have much impact on the educational value of their home environment, but they *can* teach them the tools of learning.

Please note that I am *not* suggesting that students spend half the school day playing chess, working on Rubik's Cube, or solving syllogisms in hopes of raising their IQs. Although there are those who advocate these things, I am not aware of any good evidence that such "mental exercises" raise IQs or enhance student learning. Based on the research I have seen, what students are most likely to get from playing chess every day is . . . better at playing chess. Those who work on Rubik's Cube will get better at that, and those who solve syllogisms will get better at syllogisms. If we want students to get better at learning, we must teach them skills that relate directly to learning.

What I am proposing is that teachers instruct students in specific strategies and techniques that will help them learn. There are special programs designed to teach these skills, and some of them are well worth looking into.[3] However, instruction in learning skills should be an intrinsic part of *every* lesson of the school day, not just something that is done on Tuesdays and Thursdays between 10 and 11 AM. Some of these skills (outlining and note taking, for example) are already part of the curriculum. Students are not taught to think of them as strategies to help them learn—but they should be.

There are dozens of learning skills that teachers might teach. I will limit myself here to those that seem most likely to be useful in a wide variety of situations. Although many of the skills serve more than one purpose, for the sake of convenience I will group them under three broad headings: comprehension, recall, and problem solving.

Comprehension is aided by highlighting important information. One way to do this is by taking notes. Teachers are obliged to discourage students from underlining or highlighting school texts, or from writing comments in the margin, but they can encourage students to make notes on disposable handouts or on their own paper. They can jot down important points, areas of confusion, and questions they want to ask later.

Students often listen to a presentation by a teacher or by another student, and at the conclusion they are asked if they have any questions. Typically, there are things the students didn't understand, yet they are unable to recall what questions occurred to them during their reading. Those who take notes refer to them and can get clarification. Teachers often *tell* students to take notes as they read or listen, but they seldom *teach* them how to do it.

Outlining is another way of making information comprehensible. It is particularly useful when an author has presented information in an illogical manner or when the information needs to be presented in a different order to achieve a different emphasis or objective. A biography that is not written in chronological order provides an example.

In another lifetime, when I was a magazine editor, I often had to edit material written in the style of a scholarly journal so that it would be comprehensible to normal human beings. To do this I had to figure out what the author was trying to communicate, and I did this by outlining the article. Once I had done this, I could see that the key point was A, buried on page 26 of a 50 page manuscript, that points B, C, and D were tangential to A and were included only to impress other scholars, and that points E, F, and G supported point A, while H and I were completely irrelevant. By outlining the author's original manuscript, I was able to see what he was trying to say and then produce a revised article that would make that point more clearly and succinctly.

Knowledge mapping, in which ideas are arranged on a page with lines connecting them in various ways, is a variation of outlining that some students may prefer.

Listing similarities and differences is another tool for enhancing understanding. It is a way of getting to know people, groups, organizations, and theories better. How were Abraham Lincoln and Jefferson Davis alike and different? How were the members of the French Resistance during the 1940s similar to and different from the American Colonialists who fought the British in the 1770s and 1780s? Compare (i.e., identify the similarities and differences) members of the phyla *arthropoda* and *chordata*.

Although asking students to identify similarities and differences is very useful, teachers need to do more than make this an assignment for learning a particular subject. They need to explain that this is a good way of improving understanding of almost any topic, and they need to teach students how to do it.

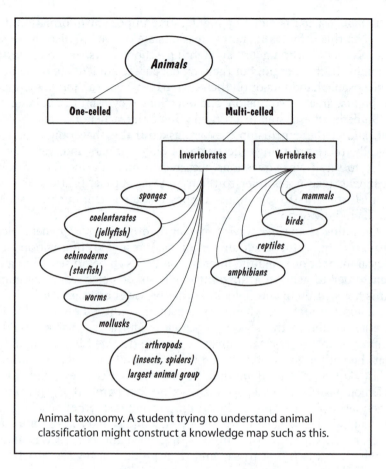

Animal taxonomy. A student trying to understand animal classification might construct a knowledge map such as this.

Thinking of analogies, metaphors, and similes is also a way of getting to know a subject better. These are really ways of asking oneself, How can I relate this new information to what I already know? For example, education students are usually required to learn the term *transfer of training*. As you may recall, this phrase means the tendency of what is learned in one situation to affect performance in a different situation. If learning to ride a motorcycle improves your ability to ride a bicycle, then we say there was transfer from the first to the second task. To better understand the transfer-of-training concept, you may have thought of the transfer slips you get on city buses, allowing you to go from one bus to another without paying an additional fare. You get an additional ride for free. In the same way, in transfer of training you get some improvement in skill for free. By making an *analogy* between bus transfers and transfer of training, you help yourself understand and remember the concept. But you weren't born knowing how to make these kinds of connections; you had to learn to do it. So do your students, and you can help them do so.

Finally, students can be taught to ask questions to improve their understanding. Often students are reluctant to do this, even when they feel hopelessly confused, because questions are treated as an admission of ignorance and may result in humiliation. The teacher who says, "If you'd been paying attention, Michael, you'd know I answered that question at the beginning of the lesson" discourages students from asking questions, including questions that were *not* answered during the lesson.

It's true that students sometimes ask questions as a way of annoying the teacher or amusing themselves, but most of the time questions reflect a genuine desire to understand something better, and that effort should be encouraged. It's important that we teach students to ask questions routinely as a way of improving their understanding.

Recall. One of the simplest ways to improve recall is to use *covert rehearsal,* which is research jargon for saying something (usually silently or *sotto voce*) over and over again. When we look up a telephone number and don't have paper and pencil, we repeat the number to ourselves until we can dial it. The practice is so common that we may forget that it is learned. But remember that Belmont and Butterfield (discussed earlier in the chapter) found that some of the kids in their study did not do covert rehearsal; they had to be taught the skill.

Students also need to be taught the value of overlearning. Most students come to understand sooner or later the value of repetition in improving recall, but many of them stop once they "know it." What's the point of continuing to recite a poem, for example, once you can do it perfectly? But as you saw in chapter 6, overlearning tends to build resistance to forgetting, and students need to be taught that it is a way of protecting the investment they have made in learning.

Another fact students need to know about improving recall is that several short study sessions are better than one or two long sessions.[4] Human nature being what it is, students are apt to put off studying. For example, they may study for an hour, or perhaps even two or three hours, the day before a test. But such cramming is less effective than studying for 15 minutes a day over a period of several days or weeks. Students need to be told that they can reduce the amount of time they spend studying by spreading it out over a long period. They can do this by studying in odd moments, such as while waiting for a school bus or when they have completed an assignment in class and have nothing to do.

One of the things students can do to make it easier to recall new information is to simplify the material, effectively reducing the amount of material they need to learn. Outlines, diagrams, graphs, and drawings are ways of imposing a structure on information that simplifies it, thereby making it easier to recall.

Acronyms are another way to reduce the amount to be recalled. Ask me to name the Great Lakes, and I will happily rattle off Huron, Ontario,

Michigan, Erie, and Superior. I can do this, not because I have a superb memory, but because somebody once told me that the first letters of the Great Lakes can be arranged to spell HOMES. As long as I can remember *that*, I can remember the Great Lakes.

Paraphrasing—restating text in one's own words—is a way of simplifying information, thereby making it easier to remember. In dividing by fractions, the teacher may say, "You invert the numerator and the denominator and then multiply." The student is apt to recall this procedure better if he recasts it as, "You put the top number on the bottom and the bottom number on the top, then multiply."

Mnemonics, such as the old rhyme, "Use i before e, except after c, and in sounding like a, as in neighbor and weigh," also make it easier to recall facts. Medical students learn the names of the twelve cranial nerves by memorizing, "On Old Olympus's towering top/a Finn and German/ vaulted and hopped." The first letter of each word corresponds to the first letter of each nerve (olfactory, optic, etc.). And we all remember the North Atlantic Treaty Organization by its acronym, NATO.

Students can also improve recall by relating new information to what they already know. A student may have trouble recalling the boating terms *port* and *starboard*. Which is the left side of the boat, and which is the right? But if they notice that *left* and *port* both have four letters, they may then remember that they "go together." Students who have trouble remembering the order of silverware when setting the table may suddenly "get it" when they realize the implements are set in alphabetical order—fork, knife, spoon.

The old information that is used to anchor new information need not have come from the classroom. Sometimes personal information can be helpful. I happen to know that Mark Twain died in 1910,

"I expect you all to be independent, innovative, critical thinkers who will do exactly as I say!"

James Warren

but I remember this only because 1910 was also the year in which my mother was born. I recall that John F. Kennedy was assassinated in the fall of 1963 because that was the year I began teaching, and I was in class when the announcement came over the intercom.

Some kinds of information are particularly helpful in improving recall of new information. For example, learning Latin word roots gives one a "leg up" in learning scientific and legal terms, which is one reason many students planning a career in law, medicine, or biology take Latin in high school. Consider the task of recalling that *pterodactyl* means any of several extinct flying reptiles. One way to learn this is to repeat it over and over. But the student who knows that *ptero* is the Latin word for wing and *dactyl* is Latin for finger also knows that *pterodactyl* literally means winged finger.[5]

Teachers make use of many of these devices to help students remember. Teaching students the *i before e* spelling rule is, for example, standard procedure. But students should be taught to use devices of this sort *on their own* as ways of helping them remember what they learn.

Problem solving. Reuven Feuerstein, the prominent Israeli psychologist who worked with underachieving children, found that they were careless and haphazard in their approach to problems.[6] Asked to identify geometric shapes by touch, for example, they hold them in their palms rather than carefully fingering them. Feuerstein taught them to use a variety of problem-solving strategies.

One strategy is *self-talk,* jargon for talking to oneself, either silently or aloud. Self-talk may seem so obvious a strategy that it need not be taught. It is, after all, largely what most of us mean when we speak of thinking. But students who have difficulty solving problems often do not talk to themselves about the problem, except perhaps to reread it. Canadian psychologist Donald Meichenbaum has shown that students can learn to do self-talk if it is demonstrated by a teacher. He and a colleague demonstrated self-talk to elementary school students by thinking aloud as they worked on a task that involved copying patterns of lines:

> Okay, what is it I have to do? I have to copy the picture with the different lines. I have to go slowly and carefully. Okay, draw the line down, down, good; and then to the right, that's it; now down some more and to the left. . . . Now back up again. No, I was supposed to go down. That's okay. Just erase the line carefully. . . . Good . . . I have to go down now. Finished. I did it![7]

Another strategy students can be taught is to *question assumptions*. It's often the case that the stumbling block in solving a problem is a false assumption. Abraham Lincoln liked to illustrate this by posing the following problem: If you call a dog's tail a leg, how many legs does it have? When a person answered, "Five," Lincoln replied that the answer was four and pointed out that calling a dog's tail a leg does not make it a leg. Many of the problems one sees in puzzle magazines are difficult mainly because they capitalize on the tendency of people to make false assumptions.

Students also need to learn when to set a problem aside for a time. Grinding away at a problem, going through the same steps and thinking the same thoughts over and over again is often ineffective. Mathematicians, scientists, and scholars who are stumped by a problem often put it aside for a week, a month, sometimes even longer. When they again turn their attention to it, they often find that the difficulty has disappeared. Many writers have also found the tactic useful. When my writing hits a snag, I clean the rain gutters.[8]

Students can't usually set a problem aside for several days or months, but even short breaks can be helpful. If a student is assigned to work on a set of problems and can't get anywhere with one of them, he can move on to another. If he is at home and gets stuck on a physics problem, he can turn his attention to a literature assignment. When he returns to the physics problem, he's more likely to see a solution.

The learning strategies reviewed here for improving comprehension, recall, and problem solving are merely a sampling of the tools teachers can and should teach their students. How do you teach learning strategies? The same way you teach history, geography, music, or anything else. The essence is to model or explain the skill, induce the student to perform it, offer feedback on her performance, and provide lots and lots of practice.

As I have said, most learning strategies are best taught not as independent subjects, but as part and parcel of reading, writing, math, science, art, and all the other subjects in the curriculum. Learning these subjects should mean learning how to understand them, how to remember them, and how to solve the problems associated with them.

The ability to learn may be something that is present in us from birth, but the strategies needed to get the most out of a learning experience must themselves be learned. These tools can be, and should be, taught. As Churchill might have said, If we give them the tools, they will get the job done.

Unfortunately, even the best-equipped students are not always angelic. Because of this, to be an effective teacher you must learn how to . . .

Deal with the Junk

> *Teachers are the only professionals who have to respond to bells every forty-five minutes and come out fighting.*
>
> —Frank McCourt

In the first few minutes of Frank McCourt's first day as a teacher, a student threw a sandwich across the classroom. This was not, McCourt knew, merely a small act of retaliation by one adolescent against another. It was a test, a test of the new teacher.[1]

McCourt, then a young man fresh out of college and as green as a lime, considered how he should respond. He later wrote:

> Professors of education at New York University never lectured on how to handle flying-sandwich situations. They talked about theories and philosophies of education, about moral and ethical imperatives, about the necessity of dealing with the whole child, the gestalt, if you don't mind, the child's felt needs, but never about critical moments in the classroom.[2]

It was, he knew, a defining moment—his credibility with the students, his ability to maintain some semblance of order, was on the line. Should he reprimand the offending student? Send him to the office? Yell at him? Smack him on the back of the head? Make him stand in the corner? Begin a discussion of classroom conduct? Give a lecture on adult behavior? Write a list of rules on the board—beginning with "No throwing of sandwiches"? What should he do?

McCourt picked up the sandwich, unwrapped it—and ate it. "It was my first act of classroom management. . . . I could see the admiration in their eyes. . . ."[3]

McCourt's story makes us smile, but it leaves us in doubt about how to handle classroom disruptions. McCourt's novel approach to the sandwich worked for him with that group of high school students, but it might not have worked for him with a group of fifth graders. And even if it had, it wouldn't give us much guidance for most of the disruptions that can occur in classrooms. What, for example, do you do when the object thrown is not a sandwich, but a paper plane, an eraser, a book, or a chair?

We all know that disruptive behavior shouldn't be a major issue in education, yet it is. A 1997 poll revealed that 58% of K–12 teachers said behavior that disrupted instruction occurred "most of the time or fairly often." The problem was worse with younger students, with 65% of elementary teachers saying that disruptions were common, but 45% of high school teachers agreed.[4]

There are disruptions, and then there are *disruptions*. When people outside the educational community hear about classroom disruptions, they often think of armed students attacking other students or teachers. While such things do happen, and these incidents do tend to capture headlines, they are rare in most schools and uncommon even in poor inner-city schools. When fights do occur, they usually involve hair pulling or fists and end with injuries no worse than black eyes and bloody noses.

Most disruptions are fairly trivial matters, what Glenn Latham called "junk behavior." They include throwing spitballs or paper planes, writing notes to or talking to another student, making inappropriate remarks or noises, teasing another student, asking questions or making comments intended to harass or embarrass the teacher, moving about the room, requesting unnecessary trips to the bathroom, leaving the room without permission, using vulgar language, and various forms of disrespect for teachers. Today, technology has added nuisances such as talking on cell phones, playing video games, and sending text messages.

As I write this, a ninth grader I had years ago comes to mind. Richard Stars always seemed to be either in trouble, or thinking of ways to get there.[5] Although I never said so publicly, I always thought of him as "Richard, send him to the stars, Stars." Yet, I was lucky. While Richard was a nuisance, his behavior never reached the level of the outrageous in my class. A colleague wasn't so fortunate. She once complained that during a lesson Richard suddenly got up and ran to the other side of the room and sat down in another seat.

"Richard," said the teacher, "return to your seat this instant!"

"I can't, Mrs. Donnely," came the reply.

"And why can't you?" demanded Mrs. Donnely.

"Because I cut a fart, and it *stinks* over there."

But while junk behavior does not threaten life or limb, it is important. Taken in isolation, minor disruptions are harmless, sometimes humorous, but each episode distracts both the students and the teacher and reduces the amount of learning that takes place. The effect of disruptions is cumulative, so a steady stream of them can seriously undermine student progress. A few Richard Stars in a class (a thought that makes me shudder, even today) can monopolize up to 90% of a teacher's attention.[6]

Frequent disruptions also are a great drain on a teacher's energy and are a major source of teacher burnout. Fear that a class will get out of control is one of the greatest concerns teachers have, especially first-year teachers.[7]

Some teachers refuse to accept responsibility for maintaining order in the classroom. "I'm a teacher," they say, "not a police officer." But what do they envisage—a police officer in the back of every classroom? ("Officer, arrest that student. He's chewing gum!") The fact is that parents, principals, and school boards have *always* expected teachers to maintain good decorum in the classroom. So do the students themselves—including the troublemakers.[8] Like it or not, maintaining order is part of the teacher's job.

We can debate the question of whom to blame for disruptive students. Some blame the students, others the parents, the mass media, society at large, and even environmental toxins. But no matter where you place the blame, the junk that occurs is still yours to deal with.[9] Junk behavior is rather like the empty beer can someone throws into your front yard during the night. It doesn't much matter where it came from, it's still your problem.

How do you get rid of classroom junk? Nobody has a perfect answer to that question, but researchers and successful teachers will generally agree, I think, about the following guidelines:

Teach well. The best way to deal with disruptive behavior is to prevent it, and the single most important thing you can do to prevent misbehavior is to teach well. That is why this chapter comes last. Developing your craft as a teacher will reduce the number of disruptions more than anything else you can do, short of coming to class wearing a karate outfit with a black belt and carrying a police officer's nightstick.

When students are actively engaged in learning tasks and making progress, they are inclined to remain engaged. This has been referred to as *instructional momentum.*[10] Think of a heavy log rolling down a hill. Once it gets going, it is hard to stop it. It has momentum. When instructional momentum is lost, it tends to stay lost. Think of that heavy log rolling downhill. If the log comes to a flat area it will stop, and once it does it takes hard labor to get it rolling again.

In the classroom, there is always something for the "logs" to do in the flat areas. If you're very, very lucky, that something might be quietly contemplating Kant's *Critique of Pure Reason* or mentally playing one of Bach's Brandenburg concertos. Unfortunately, nobody is that lucky. When your students hit a flat area—when they stop learning—it's more likely that they will contemplate the virtues of pulling someone's hair or loudly tapping a jazz drum solo on a desk with a pencil.

It's important to remember that students *always* have options. They can attend to your demonstration, do the workbook exercises, contribute to the class discussion, write the essay—or they can make jokes, pick fights, throw things, curse the teacher, stare out the window, or do any number of other things. The teacher has to make learning a more attractive option than mischief. This does not mean putting on a harlequin's costume and entertaining the troops. It means teaching so that students always know what the goal is, are always engaged, and are always making progress. The teacher's job is to keep them rolling down that hill.

Teach on your feet. One of my first insights into teaching was that there was a relationship between my posture and my students' behavior.

If I sat at my desk, student behavior deteriorated. If I stood up, behavior improved. I learned that American poet David McCord[11] knew what he was talking about when he wrote:

> The decent docent doesn't doze;
> He teaches standing on his toes.

I also noticed that geography was important. If I moved away from a student, he became more likely to get into mischief. If I moved closer, he was more attentive to work. I soon learned to stay on my feet and, when students were doing seat work, to move around the room. As master teacher Marva Collins observed, "To be a good teacher, you need a comfortable pair of shoes."[12] Most teachers learn these lessons sooner or later—though not always in their teacher training classes.

Remaining on your feet and moving about the room help reduce behavior problems for two reasons. First, problem behavior often arises when a student cannot do the assigned work. You will get a lot more questions from students who are struggling if you are moving around the room than if you are sitting at your desk. You will also know when a student is struggling, even if she doesn't ask for help, and you will be able to jump-start her efforts.

"So, other than that, how was your first day as a teacher?"

George B. Abbott

Second, problem behavior is like cancer—it's easier to treat in its earliest stages. If you are standing up, you will see the straw on the desk. If you are sitting down, you will learn about the straw when someone yelps in pain after being hit with a spitball.

Notice the good stuff. Glenn Latham told a story about how he calmed a class gone wild. He was visiting an elementary school and stepped into a classroom that looked like Wal-Mart during an 80% off sale. Children were running about the room, throwing things, laughing and shouting and—well, having a great time, really, but learning nothing. Their teacher had abandoned ship, leaving an aide helplessly sobbing as she surveyed the battlefield. Glenn approached the aide and asked if she would like his help. She fought back tears and nodded yes.

Glenn looked around the room and noticed that one of the children was sitting at his desk and not behaving quite as badly as the others. Glenn walked over to him and leaned over the student's desk. On it there was a sheet of paper with some math problems—the assignment the students had been given before MSD (mad student disease) broke out.

Glenn studied that piece of paper as if it held the deepest secrets of the universe. The boy noticed Glenn's fascination, and Glenn said, "This looks interesting. What is it?" The student explained the assignment, and Glenn asked him if he could demonstrate how to get the answers. The boy began showing Glenn how to solve the problems.

A nearby student began showing interest in what Latham and the student were doing. Glenn said to the first boy, "I'll be right back. I think this other boy needs some help." Then he went to the second student and got him started on the work. Each time he helped a student get started on the assignment, nearby students began taking an interest in it. Glenn went from student to student in this way, and in a matter of minutes the entire class was hard at work.

What did Latham do to restore order in the class? He did not shout. He did not shove any wandering student into a chair. He sent no one to the principal's office. He made no threats. All he did was show an interest in students who were engaging in something resembling appropriate behavior.

Now, I am not suggesting that the same procedure would have worked with a group of inner-city teens who were members of rival gangs and engaged in a brawl with knives and lengths of lead pipe. But there are many studies demonstrating that showing an interest in students when they behave well results in less bad behavior.[13] For example, Don Thomas and colleagues found that the level of noise and disruptive behavior in a classroom varied systematically with the teacher's behavior toward the students.[14] When teachers focused on approving appropriate student behavior, students were quiet and on-task; when teachers focused on disapproving inappropriate behavior, students became noisy and disruptive. Charles Madsen and coworkers concluded from a similar study that approving appropriate student behavior is probably the key to an orderly classroom. Notice the behavior you want, and you'll see less of the behavior you don't want.[15]

Make the good stuff pay. Sometimes simply attending to students when they behave well is not enough. If you've got students who are barely civilized, or students for whom the words *school* and *success* do not go together, you may need to offer concrete rewards for good conduct and hard work.

One way of doing this with a group of students is through a *token economy,* a system by which students receive tokens that they can later "cash in" for tangible rewards (see Appendix C). If properly used, token economies can be very effective. They can even have positive effects that endure long after the token economy ends. Donald Dickinson looked at eighth graders who had experienced a token economy in the fifth and sixth grades. He found that two years after the program ended the students were better behaved and more advanced academically than students who had not experienced a token economy.[16]

Another approach is through schoolwide programs that emphasize rewarding good behavior.[17] An example is the "Gotcha!" program in West Virginia. It provides a certificate and small prizes to students who come to class prepared, work hard, and are respectful to others. Currently used in eleven elementary and secondary schools, it has reduced violent behavior by as much as 60%. At Grandview Elementary, near Charleston, referrals to the principal for misconduct fell from 250 a year to 79.

Ignore the (small) bad stuff. A lot of behavior, particularly in elementary school students, is just normal silliness. Kids belch, giggle, drop their books, make silly remarks, and say, "Hey, look!" when something interesting happens outside the window.

You have to ask yourself whether responding to this kind of behavior will serve any useful purpose. Often the teacher's response disrupts the lesson more than the misconduct.

Punish sparingly. Some students engage in behavior that seriously interrupts the lesson and undermines students' efforts to learn. Punishment may be justified, even mandatory, in these situations. But what sort of punishment?

Some teachers send offenders to the principal's office. I never could see the point. For one thing, when you do that you are telling the principal and, more importantly, your students, "I can't do the job on my own. I need help from the Head Honcho in the front office." Is that really the message you want to send? Worse, it never seemed to me that taking this action did any good. Basically, the Principal or VP gives the student "a talking to," and lets him cool his heels on a bench until the next bell.

You're expecting a personality transplant from that? As punishment, sending students to the office is usually a flop.

Another popular punishment that seems counterproductive is assigning extra schoolwork. At one time it was commonplace to require students to write sentences such as, "I will not chew gum in class," or "I will not talk in class." Students also wrote essays on why they should not do whatever it was they had done. If there is a better way of teaching students to hate writing, I don't want to know about it.

Fortunately, there are some forms of punishment that are less problematic and more effective. Reprimands can be effective, if used properly. Proper use means no sarcasm, no insults, no degrading or humiliating remarks, just a simple statement of the student's error. A quiet word said while standing next to the student (something like, "Albert, it's rude to speak that way") is usually more effective than one broadcast across the room.[18] An angry outburst by the teacher, however, is likely to make matters worse. B. Othanel Smith writes, for example, "Research indicates that angry and punitive expressions of disapproval tend to provoke students to respond with further disruptions."[19]

If you have a good relationship with your students, they care what you think of them. When that is the case, quietly saying something like, "Bart, you really disappoint me when you curse" may sting more than a blow from a leather strap—and may do more good.

But you have to be careful with reprimands, especially public reprimands. For one thing, they can backfire by making a student the center of attention. For some students, attention is more precious than chocolate. Experiments have shown, for example, that when young students are reprimanded for misbehavior, misbehavior sometimes *increases*. In other words, reprimands can be rewarding.[20]

One of the most popular forms of punishment in schools today is *time out*—an abbreviation for *time out from positive reinforcement*. As the name suggests, time out consists of moving a child from a rewarding situation to an unrewarding situation for a *short* period (usually no more than five minutes). The time-out zone is often a small area in one corner of the classroom separated from the class by an opaque or translucent screen. The area should include a chair and as little else as possible: No texts, workbooks, magazines, computers, pictures on the wall, and no contact with the teacher or other students.

Properly used, time out can be very effective. Unfortunately, what passes for time out in many classrooms is time out in name only. Some teachers assign students to a time-out zone that is more appealing than the rest of the classroom. Another mistake some teachers make is to go into the time-out area and chat with the student about his or her conduct. This provides attention and interest. Why anyone would think this "punishment" would result in better behavior is a mystery. If the time-out area isn't boring, then it isn't time out, it's time *in*.

Other teachers make the mistake of assigning a student to time out for a half hour or longer. There is no evidence that long periods of time out are better than very short periods.

Even properly administered time out can backfire if it provides a way for a student to escape an unpleasant situation. For example, a student may misbehave as you are about to start a math lesson if math is scary for him, or he may misbehave to avoid collaborative work if he is assigned to work with (ugh!) a girl! In the same way, students will get themselves "sent" to the office if that is a way of avoiding embarrassment.

Another effective form of punishment is *overcorrection*. The idea here is to take the position that the student has made an error and needs practice in performing correctly. The student who slams a door, for example, is immediately required to close the door properly not once, but three or four times. Overcorrection has been studied in school settings, and it usually gets good results. To use this form of punishment successfully, however, you often need to stand near the student, tell her what she is to do, and stay with her while she does it.

Another procedure is called *self-instruction*. It consists of standing near the student and asking him what he should have done:

TEACHER: John, what answer did you get to the problem?

JOHN: Man, I don't know how to do this shit.

TEACHER (approaches and speaks softly directly to John): John, that kind of language is not acceptable. How should you have answered my question?

JOHN: All I said was . . .

TEACHER: I know what you said. What *should* you have said?

JOHN (with a smirk): "I don't know how to do this crap?" (A few chuckles are heard from nearby students.)

TEACHER (unfazed, and ignoring the laughter): What *should* you have said, John?

JOHN (shrugging): I guess, "I didn't get the answer."

TEACHER (without sarcasm): Excellent. (Speaking more loudly) Bill, what answer did you get?

When students are asked to say what they should have done, they are later more likely to behave in that way.[21]

In exchanges with students about misbehavior, it's important to avoid getting into a debate or argument with the student. This rarely goes well:

TEACHER: John, what answer did you get to the problem?

JOHN: Man, I don't know how to do this shit.

TEACHER (addressing John from across the room): John, that kind of language is not acceptable.

JOHN: All I said was . . .

TEACHER: I know what you said. But I don't want your garbage mouth in my classroom.

JOHN: Well, I don't wanna be in your garbage classroom.

TEACHER: This classroom is better than you deserve.

JOHN: Fine. Then I'll go someplace else. (Rises and heads for the door.)

TEACHER (shouting): Sit down!

JOHN (shouting): Go to hell, you @#%$! (Slams the door on his way out.)

Calmly asking the student to state what he should have done avoids this kind of unpleasant and counterproductive exchange. A teacher never really wins an argument with a student. If the student comes out ahead, the teacher's credibility is damaged. If the teacher comes out ahead, the losing student will find a way to get revenge.

Corporal punishment has to be mentioned, since many people think it is *the* solution to behavior problems. The term corporal (or physical) punishment refers to any kind of punishment that causes physical discomfort. It includes hair pulling, pinching, slapping, caning, and (perhaps worst of all) shaking. However, in American schools, the only sanctioned form of corporal punishment is usually paddling—striking the child on the buttocks with a wooden paddle.

As I write this, paddling is legal in 21 states. It is usually administered by the principal, but in some states the teacher is allowed to paddle. Its use is not rare. Over a quarter of a million public school students were paddled by teachers or school staff in the 2004–2005 school year, the latest for which statistics are available.[22] In addition, some teachers use other forms of physical punishment, such as pinching or shaking, on their own initiative. Since these instances are not routinely recorded, there is no way to know how much pain is inflicted on children in the name of discipline. Whatever it is, it's too much.

It has to be admitted that corporal punishment can be effective if properly used, but this does not necessarily justify its use. Even from a strictly practical point of view, the costs often outweigh the benefits.

What are the costs of corporal punishment?[23] An obvious one is the risk of physical injury. Shaking, for example, can cause neck and brain injury, particularly in small children.[24] Paddling sometimes causes serious permanent injuries. Even pinching can break blood vessels, and slapping can break bones.

A natural consequence of corporal punishment is fear of those who administer the punishment. This can result in "ditching" school or dropping out. And a fearful climate is unlikely to inculcate a love of learning. Another consequence is retaliation. Students get even by stealing, committing acts of vandalism, and sometimes through violence.[25] Finally, there is the risk of psychological damage. Children are remarkably resilient, but physical punishment in school of a child who is being abused at home may increase the risk of depression or other psychological disorders. Even children who are not abused at home might develop problems such as chronic anxiety.

There are people who mean well and who genuinely believe that corporal punishment is essential to maintaining good discipline. But in my opinion, physical punishment cannot be justified for controlling classroom misconduct—even persistent, highly disruptive misconduct. Fortunately, the alternatives to physical punishment discussed earlier are nearly always effective.

The guidelines just offered should help you maintain decorum in your classroom. I can assure you that if you follow them faithfully, you will have fewer disruptions. I can also assure you that even if you follow them faithfully, you will still have *some* disruptions. If you want some magic words that will cast a spell over students so they never misbehave, write to Harry Potter. Maybe he can help you. I can't. Junk behavior is and always has been part of the teacher's life because kids are, well . . . kids. But following the guidelines offered here can make the difference between a day that leaves you smiling and one that leaves you banging your head against a wall.

In this book, you've read about what I believe are the essential elements of effective teaching. But becoming an effective teacher is not something you achieve simply by reading about it. You must study, get expert advice, practice, and change in accordance with the results you get. You must work at it constantly, always striving to improve, always working to master what no one has ever truly mastered: *the teacher's craft*.

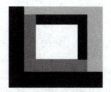

Epilogue
What's the Point?

> *Nothing worth doing is completed in our lifetime; therefore, we must be saved by hope.*
>
> —Reinhold Niebuhr

After I had written the manuscript for this book, I sent a copy to a friend for comment. By reply he sent a newspaper article describing the sorry state of schools in the city where he lives—poor academic achievement, fights in school, high dropout rates, and the involvement of students with drugs and gangs. My friend's accompanying note said, in effect, "I wish fixing this mess were as simple as merely improving teaching, but it isn't."

His comment troubled me, since he seemed to have missed the point of my book. Somehow he thought I was suggesting that if we could just get teachers to teach more effectively, all of the problems in our schools, and perhaps outside them as well, would disappear.

I had intended to suggest nothing of the sort. My goals were, and are, far more modest. But since you might also interpret this work as my friend did, I will attempt to clarify my views on the value of effective teaching.

I am not under the illusion that this or any other book will spark a revolution in education, and that large numbers of teachers will suddenly adopt the kind of evidence-based instruction described in the preceding chapters. Even if that were to happen, I know of no reason to believe that effective teaching alone would eradicate crime, drug abuse, child pornography, and teen pregnancy, any more than it would prevent cancer, cure acne, or ensure that every teenager in the country will have a date for the senior prom. So I am *not* suggesting that effective teaching will solve all of our society's problems, or even solve all of the problems in our schools.

What I *am* suggesting is that there is a body of evidence that shows quite clearly how to teach so that students will learn far more than they are learning today. I fully believe that if we were to teach in this way from kindergarten through grade twelve with all students, the results would be astounding.

But I said "if," and it is a very big *if*. I wish I could believe that, at some point in the not-too-distant future, what is now possible would become reality, but I don't. In truth, I think it will be a long time coming. I don't expect to see it in my lifetime, and you may not see it in yours.

This is, I realize, a depressing way to end a book. "If things are so gloomy," you may be thinking, "if effective methods of instruction are not going to be widely accepted any time soon, then why should I go to the trouble of teaching in the most effective way? What's the point?"

Good question. I will answer in the form of a parable.[1]

Two friends are walking along a beach in southern California. It is summer, and the grunion are running. The grunion is a small fish, a kind of smelt. For four days every summer the grunion swim onto southern California beaches to spawn, and many become stranded and die.

As the men walk along the beach, many of the fish lay at their feet, gasping for air. One of the men picks up a fish and hurls it as far out to sea as he can. He hopes that with his help, the fish might get past the breakers and make its way to safety. He picks up another fish, and throws it into the sea. He does this again and again.

His friend smiles at the effort. "Look," he finally says, "there are thousands of fish stranded here on the beach. What you're doing won't make any difference."

His companion picks up another fish, admires it for a moment, then hurls it as far as he can into the sea. Then he says, "It makes a difference to *that* fish."

If you work very hard and become the best teacher you can be, it will make no difference to thousands of students left stranded by a troubled society and a troubled educational system.

But it will make a *huge* difference to *your* students.

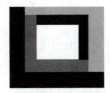

Recommended Reading

I list below (in alphabetical order) several books that I think will be helpful to any teacher, but especially to those who are new to the field. Some of these books are easy-to-read, down-to-earth, practical guides that offer advice based on the author's classroom experience. Other books are more scholarly, and they underline the fact that there is a body of data on which effective teaching can be based. All are worth reading by anyone who is serious about mastering the craft of teaching.

Esmé Raji Codell
Educating Esmé
Chapel Hill, NC: Algonquin Books, 2001
> The diary of a teacher's first year in the classroom. Codell makes us smile while showing us the difficulties, frustrations, disappointments, and pleasures of teaching.

Thomas L. Good and Jere E. Brophy
Looking in Classrooms (8th edition)
New York: Longman, 2000
> This is the only text on my list, and, like most college texts, it is not the sort of book you want to curl up with in your hammock on a summer's day. However, it is a scholarly review of instructional research by two prominent educational researchers and serves as an excellent reference. It ought to be on every teacher's bookshelf as a resource. Since it is revised regularly, be sure to get the latest edition.

Rafe Esquith
There Are No Shortcuts
New York: Pantheon Books, 2003
> A well-written, first-rate look at day-to-day work by a dedicated teacher. Esquith's characters are "composites," so this is a fictionalized account, but the kinds of frustrations, failures, and successes he describes are real enough.

Kent Johnson and Elizabeth M. Street
The Morningside Model of Generative Instruction: What It Means to Leave No Child Behind
Concord, MA: Cambridge Center for Behavioral Studies, 2004

Morningside Academy is a private school in Seattle, Washington, founded and directed by Kent Johnson. The school admits students who are at least two grade levels behind in reading and/or math based on standardized achievement tests. Many of the students have been labeled amotivated, slow learners, or ADHD (having attention deficit/ hyperactive disorder). The school *guarantees* that students will gain two grade levels in reading and math in one school year—or the school will refund their tuition. In 30 years, Morningside has never had to refund money. In this book, Johnson and Street describe the highly successful Morningside approach.

Fred H. Jones
Tools for Teaching: Discipline, Instruction, Motivation
Santa Cruz, CA: Fredric H. Jones & Associates, Inc., 2000

This is mainly a nitty-gritty guide to classroom management. It may strike some readers as focusing too much on "controlling" students, but it offers many practical suggestions on preventing and dealing with various kinds of classroom mischief. The book is loaded with aphorisms such as, "The standards in any classroom are defined by whatever students can get away with."

Glenn Latham
Behind the Schoolhouse Door: Eight Skills Every Teacher Should Know
Logan, UT: Mountain Plains Regional Resource Center, Utah State University, 1997

The late Glenn Latham was a teacher, counselor, researcher, and educational consultant. Those who knew him remember him as one of the warmest, most caring people they've ever met. Fortunately, he was also an excellent writer. In this small, little known but quite readable book, he discusses eight skills he considers central to effective teaching.

Glenn Latham
Keys to Classroom Management
Logan, UT: Parents & Teachers ink, 1998

Glenn's style of classroom management was simple, elegant, and humane. He believed in neither being lord and master over students, nor letting them be his lords and masters. His tools were mutual respect, clear expectations, recognition of appropriate behavior, and an ability to avoid the traps kids set for unwary adults. Teachers (and parents) who have sworn the only way to deal with kids is to *"make* them behave" have found life easier after trying the Latham approach.

Frank McCourt
Teacher Man
New York: Scribner, 2005

McCourt won the Pulitzer Prize for *Angela's Ashes,* a memoir about growing up in Ireland. *Teacher Man* is about his work as a teacher. I am not at all sure that McCourt was as good a teacher as he is a writer, but he does show that much of a teacher's education takes place on the job.

Cathy L. Watkins
Project Follow Through: A Case Study of Contingencies Influencing Instructional Practices of the Educational Establishment
Cambridge, MA: Cambridge Center for Behavioral Studies, 1997

If you want to know why the largest, most expensive educational experiment in the history of the world has been almost completely ignored despite revealing quite clearly what instructional approaches work best, then there is no better place to look.

Harry K. Wong and Rosemary T. Wong
The First Days of School: How to Be an Effective Teacher
Mountain View, CA: Harry K. Wong Publications, Inc., 2001

According to the authors, this book has sold more than 500,000 copies, which may make it the best-selling "how to" teaching book in print. In addition to sensible advice ("Stand up when you address the class, and speak in short, clear sentences or phrases."), the authors include useful suggestions and comments from practicing teachers.

Appendix A
Item Analysis: Assessing the Test

A paper-and-pencil test is only as good as its individual items, but how can you tell if a test item is good?

One procedure is to have the students vote on it. As you go over the test, students will complain that this or that item was confusing or ambiguous. The teacher then asks, 'How many think number 4 was a bad question?' Whereupon, of course, every one who got number 4 wrong raises his or her hand. If there are a lot of hands in the air, the teacher throws out the item.

A variation of this procedure is to anticipate the vote. After the teacher scores the tests, she counts the number of students who got each item wrong. She then discards those items that a lot of students missed.

Although I have seen professors with doctorates in psychology use these methods, neither has any basis in logic. An item missed by a lot of students is not necessarily a bad item; it may be simply a difficult item. There is no reason why a test should not have some difficult items, and throwing out difficult items unfairly penalizes the more knowledgeable students. Logic would have the teacher discard difficult items only if they are also *bad* items. A simple procedure that identifies bad test items is called *item analysis*.

Item analysis rests on the assumption that the more a student knows about a topic, the more likely he or she is to answer any given question on that topic correctly—unless the item is flawed. A bad test item, then, is one that students who know very little are as likely to answer correctly as students who know a lot.

To do an item analysis, first arrange the tests in order of total scores and divide them into three stacks: top third, middle third, bottom third. Make sure the top and bottom thirds have the same number of tests in them. Now list all of the test items by number on a sheet of paper. Next, draw a vertical line down the middle of the page to create two columns and label them top one-third and bottom one-third. Go through one of the tests in the top third and put a slash mark in the first column next to every item that student answered correctly. Do the same thing with all tests in the top third. Now repeat the procedure for tests in the bottom third, but make slash marks in the second column.

When you have done this, look over the data for each item. Good items will be answered correctly by more students in the top third than in the bottom third. An item that is answered correctly by about as many students in the top and bottom thirds is a very questionable item and probably should be eliminated. If more students in the bottom third answer a question correctly than students in the top third do, that item definitely should be discarded.

item	top third	bottom third
1.	卅 ///	卅
2.	卅	卅 /
3.	///	
4.	///	卅 /

Item analysis. Question 1 appears to be a good item, but fairly easy. Item 2 is highly questionable. Item 3 is a good item, but rather difficult. Item 4 is definitely a bad item since the students who knew least about the subject were more likely to answer correctly than those who knew most. (There are 8 students in each third.)

Doing an item analysis for 30 objective items taken by 30 students may take about half an hour. If you have 150 students (100 test papers to analyze) the investment of time is considerable. However, if you give the same test to all 150 students, you can reduce the labor involved by randomly selecting 15 tests from the top and bottom thirds—30 test papers—and analyzing them. This sample will yield essentially the same results as analyzing all 100 tests.

Item analysis is the only way of determining which items are truly assessing what students have learned. I always explain to students how I did the item analysis, so that they know I made a conscientious effort to remove bad items in a fair way. Often I print out a table showing the item analysis and distribute it to students before I explain the procedure. Doing this greatly reduces the amount of wheedling and complaints of unfairness by students. It also demonstrates a practical application of mathematics.

Item analysis is not applicable to essay questions and other subjectively scored items. It works very well, however, with objective test items such as multiple-choice, fill-in-the-blank, completion, matching, and the like. With such items, it provides a simple and fair way of assessing the test.

Appendix B
Grades

Assessment, according to the view that I have advocated, has little if anything to do with grades. Grades are fundamentally about ranking students, not about deciding what they need to learn. Nevertheless, grades are a fact of educational life, so I feel obliged to consider the topic.

There are two basic ways of assigning a grade on a test or, for that matter, anything else. One is to grade "on the curve," and the other is to grade against a standard.

To grade on the curve means to assign a certain percentage of As, Bs, and so on, regardless of the scores obtained. For example, a teacher may decide to give As to the top 10% of students, Bs to the next 20%, Cs to the middle 40%, Ds to the next 20%, and Fs to the bottom 10%. Grading is "on the curve" in the sense that the teacher distributes grades as though the student scores were distributed on a normal bell curve.

This approach runs into problems in small classes, among other places. If a teacher has five students, for example, then what does she do—give the top score an A, the next a B, and so on? If scores bunch up, this also causes problems. If a teacher has 30 students and 15 of them score 95% or higher, how can she give 10% of the students As? What if the lowest score in class is 85? Should the students who score 85 get Fs simply because they are at the bottom of the curve? In theory, the more successful the teacher is, the more students with high scores would receive failing grades. I'm not sure I see how this motivates anyone, teacher or student, to do better.

Teachers get around these problems by using "natural groupings" of scores to assign grades. Unfortunately, deciding what is a natural grouping is a subjective matter, and different teachers can come up with very different grade assignments.

Sometimes the natural groupings force instructors to make rather bizarre distinctions. In the scores shown on the following page, for example, there is a big gap between the lowest A score and the highest B

Instructor 1	Instructor 2	Instructor 3
98 ⎫	98 ⎫	98 ⎫ A
97 ⎬ A	97 ⎬ A	97 ⎭
89 ⎪	89 ⎪	89 ⎫
85 ⎭	85 ⎭	85 ⎪
		75 ⎪
75 ⎫	75 ⎫	75 ⎬ B
75 ⎪	75 ⎪	75 ⎪
73 ⎬ B	73 ⎪	73 ⎪
70 ⎭	70 ⎪	70 ⎭
	69 ⎬ B	
69 ⎫	65 ⎪	69 ⎫
65 ⎪	63 ⎪	65 ⎪
63 ⎬ C	63 ⎭	63 ⎬ C
63 ⎭		63 ⎪
	59 ⎫	59 ⎭
59 ⎫	54 ⎪	
54 ⎪	54 ⎬ C	54 ⎫
54 ⎬ D	54 ⎪	54 ⎪
54 ⎪	50 ⎪	54 ⎬ D
50 ⎭	49 ⎭	50 ⎪
		49 ⎭
49 F		

Grading on the curve. Three different instructors might assign different grades to the same scores, though all three are using "natural groupings."

score, but in two classes there is only a one-point difference between the lowest B and the highest C.

I have heard grading on the curve described as "The only fair way to assign grades," but I see nothing fair about it. Students have no way of knowing what the standard is, since the standard depends on how well other students do. Grading on the curve discourages the better students from doing their best, since they then come under pressure from other students for being "curve busters" who make the rest of the students look bad. It discourages the weaker students from trying harder, since even if they improve, they are likely to remain near the bottom.

Grading on the curve also pits student against student instead of against ignorance, the true enemy. And it gives a relativistic notion of what constitutes achievement. Doing well comes to mean nothing more than doing better than other students, even if everyone does poorly. Grading on the curve is a sham; it pretends that absolute performance does not matter, when we all know it does.

The more honest approach is to set a standard for each letter grade, such as 90% for an A, 80% for a B, and so on, and then assign grades accordingly. This ends grade rationing and replaces it with something rational. There's now no limit on how many people can do well. If most students do well, and that should always be our hope, then they will all get high grades. If most students do poorly, then most will get low grades.

The latter is seen as a cause for panic by some teachers. "I can't give 80% of my students Ds and Fs!" they exclaim. Well, why not? If the test is of reasonable difficulty, and students receive Ds and Fs, they will work harder next time.

Unfortunately, in practice any teacher who gives low grades to a large number of students is apt to be in trouble with school administrators.

Principals tend to think that low grades make them look bad, and they object to receiving phone calls from complaining parents. However, if the standards are low in your school, you can deal with this by gradually raising your standards until you get to a level you find acceptable.

Students have become accustomed to being graded on the curve and will assume that you are going to toss the standards aside if the scores pile up at the bottom. Once, when a student complained because I did not grade on the curve, I pointed out that I had warned about that at the beginning of the course. "Yes, I know," she replied, "but all our teachers say that, and then they grade on the curve when the scores are low." Once the students realized I was the exception to the rule, they dug a little deeper and their grades came up.

Of course, it is possible to create a test that is too difficult (or too easy) for the students being tested. Inexperienced teachers in particular may overestimate or underestimate what students can accomplish. But there is an easy solution to this problem. Ask other teachers to show you their tests on the same material, or show them a copy of your test before you administer it. Either of these steps should keep your tests close to the mark. After you give the test, do an item analysis (see Appendix A) and eliminate bad items.

Grading means more than assigning a letter grade to a test or other student product. It means coming up with an overall grade that goes on the student's report card at the end of each term. To do that, you need some sort of grading system.

The traditional grading system consists of entering letter grades in a grade book and then averaging them. This system has one great advantage: simplicity. It has the disadvantage of being tedious. Averaging the grades A, B, and C is easy, but if you have a long string of grades (as you should, since you should be doing frequent formal assessments), then it becomes more troublesome. If you record numerical grades or convert letter grades to numbers, you can do the math with a calculator or grading software. Just be sure you always back up your data so your records don't evaporate into cyberspace.

A very different approach is the point system. Each test, quiz, oral report, and so on is assigned a certain number of points, and student grades for the term are based on the total number of points each student obtains.

Let us say that the total number of points available is 1000. To receive an A, the student must earn, say, 900 points (90% of the total); a B is 800 points, and so on. All points have equal value. It makes no difference whether a point comes from a quiz, an exam, an oral report, a graphic display, performance in a skit, or contributions to class discussions.

Many teachers give points for extra-credit work, but I think this is generally a mistake; it allows students to substitute busy work for learning. Students have learned that they can slide and then at the end of a term say, "I know I really neglected my work this term, but I've learned my lesson. How about if I do some extra-credit work?" Allowing them to do so merely makes the problem worse.

You'll need to keep track of the students' points in a ledger (or software), of course, but you should also require students to keep track of their points. I have students create a graph on which they record the total number of points earned as of a given date. Periodically I check these cumulative records, as they are called, and assign points if they are accurate and complete.

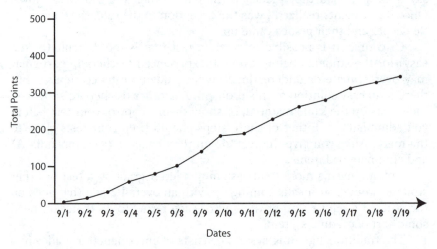

Cumulative record of points earned. Each day's earned points are added to the previous day's total and plotted on the graph. The student may periodically earn additional points for maintaining a record that is accurate and up-to-date.

Having students keep cumulative records of earned points accomplishes two things. First, the students always know how they are doing, both in terms of how much they are learning and in terms of the grade they are likely to get for the term. This relieves anxiety and reduces procrastination. In my experience, students keeping a cumulative record of the points they have earned rarely if ever say, "Gee, I didn't realize I was doing so poorly."

Second, the exercise of keeping a cumulative record is a useful learning experience. Students are collecting data, plotting it on a graph, and interpreting it. They are using science and math to monitor their progress.

I have used a point system with secondary and college students. Most preferred it to the letter-averaging system because they always knew exactly where they stood grade-wise. Some people will suggest that this puts too much stress on grades, but I think, on the contrary, that it allows the student to put grades aside. Students know where they stand, so they don't have to worry about it. I do not know if a point system has been used with elementary students, but I know of no reason why it could not be used at least as early as third grade.

I am one of many who would like to see grades abolished. However, simply announcing an end to grades within the current educational system is not workable. Grades can be abolished only if we adopt a system that allows each student to meet concrete standards at his or her own pace. One system for doing this is Fred Keller's Personalized System of Instruction, or PSI.[1]

In PSI, students advance to Unit 2 as soon as (but only if) they have mastered Unit 1. A student's permanent record shows the date on which he or she mastered (by, for example, scoring 80% or better on a unit test) each unit. Under such a system, grades become completely irrelevant. What matters is what units the student has mastered. The brightest students will, of course, complete more units per year than the slowest ones, but even the slowest students can complete sufficient units for graduating from high school by age 18. Students who fall behind schedule for that target can be given additional instruction as needed.

Unfortunately, the transition from the current lockstep system to PSI (or any self-paced system) would be a severe jolt. Sadly, I do not think self-paced instruction will be widely adopted in this country for many years.

Appendix C
The Token Economy

An excellent way of improving academic work and/or reducing misbehavior is to set up a token economy.

A token is something that has value only because it can be exchanged for something else of value. Money, for example, is a widely used token. A token economy is a micro-economy in which students earn currency of some sort (the tokens) that they can exchange for other things they value, such as school supplies (pencils, notepads, erasers), personal items (combs, berets, key chains), small toys (tops, crossword puzzles), and reading material (comic books, paperback novels). These items should be age appropriate and safe, of course, and not apt to be used inappropriately in the classroom (water guns are off the list) or items that are likely to raise parental objections (racy magazines). One way to get ideas for items is to notice what kids spend their money on; another is to ask them for suggestions.

The number of tokens required to buy each item may be set according to the actual cost of the item or by its expected value to the student. A $1 comic book might have a higher token price than a $1 notebook, for example. Prices should be set for at least one marking period, after which they might be adjusted according to market demands.

Tokens can be made by printing up slips of paper and marking them with a unique stamp purchased in a stationery or craft store. If you are handy, you can even make your own stamp from a block of wood. A distinctive mark reduces the risk of counterfeiting.

When introducing a token economy, there is no need to go into great detail. You might make a list of the items available and the price (in tokens) of each and post it in the room. Let the students know that they can earn tokens by behaving well and working hard. Suggest that the tokens are more like bonuses than salary, and that they should not expect to receive a token every class period, even if they behave very well or learn a lot. (One reason for this is, you don't want to spend half your time handing out tokens.) If you want to emphasize academic learning, you might let students earn one token for every grade of A they receive or, if you use a point system for grades, you might provide one token for every 100 points earned.

In the early days of the program, you may want to be fairly generous with tokens so that the students can see the program working. Let the students know that you will be particularly looking for improvement in behavior, and rewarding that. That way Little Miss Perfect will understand why you have given three tokens to Mugs and only one to her. From time to time, you might provide a token to all students in the class when the class as a whole has done remarkably well.

Any change in the value of tokens should be gradual, and is best done at the end of a six-week marking period. A rapid increase in the number of tokens required to buy items is apt to be resented by students, who will rightly see it as a violation of the implied contract underlying the economic system. The money for reward items is apt to come from your own pocket, so when you buy items keep in mind that you will need to replenish the supply from time to time.

When a token economy is administered correctly and consistently, it usually produces a marked improvement in behavior. But, like everything else, token economies have limitations. Probably the most serious weakness is that tokens can be lost or stolen. One way to deal with these problems is to devise a banking system. When students have earned tokens, they deposit them in the bank by giving them to the teacher or a student who records the deposit in a ledger and then puts the tokens into a locked box to which only the teacher has a key. This a great way for students to learn about banking and to make practical use of arithmetic skills. Students can record their deposits in a bank book so they always know how many tokens they have in their account.

You can even go so far as to have students create checkbooks, which you then "print" on a photocopier or computer. Then students can buy items by writing checks. You will have to charge students a penalty for writing bad checks, just as a bank would do.

Another limitation of the token economy is that it is not appropriate for all students. The very youngest students, for example, will have trouble grasping the concept. Token economies have been used successfully in the upper elementary grades and with teens, but children from well-to-do homes may smirk at the items a teacher can offer. If you have some doubt about how students will take to the program, you might introduce it as something to be tried for a six-week term as a way of learning about economic principles. Then, if the students like it, you can extend its use.

Notes

Prologue

[1] In these studies, the researchers do not assign students systematically to good and bad teachers. Rather, the researchers examine the progress of students and determine, after the fact, which teachers were effective and which were ineffective.

[2] Sanders & Rivers (1996). The effective teachers were those who were, based on the progress of their students, in the top 20% of teachers. The ineffective teachers were those who were in the bottom 20%.

[3] Jordan et al. (1997).

[4] Sanders & Horn (1998). One of the current fads in education is looping. This means that the student has the same teacher for up to five consecutive years. The evidence clearly indicates that this practice will be disastrous for those students who get stuck with a bad teacher.

[5] Haycock (1998). See also Barr & Dreeben (1983). However, it is well known that poor and minority students get more than their fair share of ineffective teachers. Bridges (1996) found that weak teachers get transferred out of middle-class white schools and into poor minority schools.

[6] "What we've consistently found," Sanders said in an interview, "starting back in the early '80s, is that when compared to class size or the ethnicity of students, or whether they're on free or reduced-price lunches, all of those things pale in comparison to the effectiveness of the individual classroom teacher" (quoted in Berg, 1998, p.1). See also Sanders & Horn (1998) and Sanders et al. (1997). The work of Sanders and others on teacher effectiveness is extremely important, but others have long recognized the importance of teachers. See, for example, Brophy & Good (1986).

[7] E.g., Bahrick & Phelps (1987).

[8] See, for example, Hopkins & Conard (1975); Lipsey & Wilson (1993); Johnson & Layng (1992); Rosenshine & Stevens (1986); Sanders & Horn (1994); Stevens & Duffy (2000).

[9] In 1988, Escalante received the Presidential Citizen's Medal from President Reagan. In 1996, with the arrival of a new principal at Garfield High, Escalante offered to return to the school and rebuild its math program. His offer was rejected. In 2001, Escalante returned to Bolivia. For more on Escalante, see Mathews (1988) or go to www.boliviaweb.com/hallfame/escalante.htm. The decline in the math program at Garfield may not have been due entirely to the departure of Escalante and Jimenez. Good teachers need the support of good administrators.

[10] For more information on Marva Collins, see Collins & Tamarkin (1982). Reuven Feuerstein (1980) is an Israeli psychologist who developed an intensive form of tutoring used with underachieving children. For a brief introduction to Feuerstein's work, see Chance (1981).

[11] The 40,000 figure comes from Hattie & Purdie (2000).

153

[12] Rosenthal & Jacobson (1968).

[13] Sociologist Robert Merton (1948) introduced the concept of self-fulfilling prophecy.

[14] For a summary of this work, see Rosenthal (1973). For a more technical discussion, see Harris & Rosenthal (1985). Not surprisingly, negative expectations have effects analogous to those of positive expectations. When teachers are led to believe that a student has limited ability, they cover less material, require fewer responses, provide less feedback, and treat the students more coolly. The students, who again have been picked at random and are not especially slow, typically learn less than other students. Rosenthal's work has been criticized; for a review of the criticisms and his replies, see Rosenthal (1995).

[15] Johnson & Layng (1992). For more on the highly effective Morningside Model, see Johnson & Layng (2004); Johnson & Street (2004).

[16] The dominant school of thought in schools of education is what might be called the minimalist model. This is the view that the teacher who does the least does the best job. The teacher "frees" the students so that they can learn on their own. The trouble with the minimalist approach is that it is generally not effective (Kirschner et al., 2006).

Chapter 1

[1] See, for example, Soar & Soar (1979); Haertel et al. (1981); Schunk & Meece (1992); and Fraser (1986, 1994).

[2] There have been many instances—school shootings, fires, earthquakes, floods—in which teachers have risked life and limb to protect the children in their care.

[3] Heaviside et al. (1998). This is not to say that student misbehavior in schools is not a problem. Nearly half of parents and two-thirds of teachers say that it is (Parents, teachers agree . . ., February 9, 2006). We will visit this subject again in chapter 10.

[4] *Public Agenda* (May, 2004).

[5] Mendell & Heath (2004).

[6] Generally, a newspaper article or a short segment on the 6 o'clock news about hazardous conditions in a school is far more likely to get action than letters of protest to administrators from a teacher. No educational administrator likes bad press. You don't know any reporters? Read the local papers and watch local news to see who covers education topics, then pick up the phone. You can also rub elbows with education reporters at Board of Education meetings and other events they are likely to cover. If you are concerned about whistle-blower retaliation, call the reporter from a pay phone and don't give your name.

[7] Earthman (2002).

[8] Collins & Tamarkin (1982), p. 50.

[9] Seymour and Seymour (1992) write that "good teachers . . . establish rules and routines early on in the school year and then—and this is the most important part—actively and consistently follow them up" (p. 100).

[10] Phillips & Smith (1992).

[11] Sternberg (2003). There are many reasons why students are generally not as respectful toward teachers as they were in decades past. However, it's possible that one reason has to do with the change in teacher attire. There is a rationale for exempting those who teach physical education, shop, and perhaps art. Science teachers on field trips to swamps may also be exempted.

[12] Madsen et al. (1970).

[13] Beaman & Wheldall (2000). Other research suggests that many parents are subject to the same negative bias; see Hart & Risley (1995), who found that the parents of children who have the least going for them typically provide very negative ratios, whereas well-educated, middle-class parents typically provide a positive ratio.

[14] Not only does a shift to the positive improve the learning climate, but numerous studies have shown that commenting favorably on desirable behavior often results in less *unde-*

sirable behavior. See, for example, Beaman & Wheldall (2000), Elliott & Busse (1991), Hart et al. (1964), McNamara (1987).

15 Latham (1992).

16 Latham (1997), p. 8.

17 Latham could offer no solid proof that an 8:1 ratio was ideal. It's possible that a ratio of 7:1 or 5:1 or even 2:1 will get results every bit as good as 8:1. We simply don't know. One thing is certain: The positives should outnumber the negatives, and all too often they do not. The results are student misconduct and a poor climate for learning.

18 See Slavin (1983; 1994). Hattie and Purdie (2000) note that cooperative forms of learning improve the ability of students to understand others' views and increase tolerance for different ethnic groups. However, there are potential problems with cooperative learning (see Mathews, 1992).

19 Aronson et al. (1978); Aronson & Patnoe (1997); Aronson (2000).

20 Gage & Berliner (1984); Brophy & Good (1970); Jussim (1989); Trujillo (1986).

21 Childress (1998), p. 618.

22 Bradley (1997). Students prefer teachers who are enthusiastic, but modest levels of teacher enthusiasm may be best. See McKinney & Larkin (1982); McKinney et al. (1984); Patrick et al. (2000).

23 Banner & Cannon (1997), p. 44. See also Banner & Cannon (April, 1997).

24 Skinner (1968) wrote: "Will machines replace teachers? On the contrary, they are . . . to be used by teachers to save time and labor. In assigning certain mechanizable functions to machines, the teacher emerges in his proper role as an indispensable human being." (p. 55).

25 Disposable cameras are ideal for this. Digital cameras are more complicated, which means you'll spend more time explaining how to use yours. Digital cameras are also more expensive. If a student drops a disposable camera, at worst you're out $10. You can have the film developed in an hour or two, so the delay is inconsequential.

26 For a brief introduction to this work, see Rosenthal et al. (1974).

27 It's also the case that *teachers* convey messages nonverbally to their students, and sometimes these messages are not very helpful. Worse, many teachers are unaware that they are sending signals such as racial bias or low expectations. College classes in nonverbal communication ought to be a regular part of teacher training. Charles Galloway (1968) suggested as much long ago (see also O'Hair & Ropo [1994]), but so far as I know such courses are seldom offered and never required of teacher trainees. Paul Ekman (2007) is the acknowledged leader in facial expressions of emotions. For a brief introduction to Ekman's work, see Foreman (2003). Rosenthal (2002) provides a brief overview of covert communication, and Knapp and Hall (2005) offer a college text on the subject.

28 Mobbs et al. (2003).

29 Turner et al. (2002). See also Provine (2000), who notes that "harried people don't laugh much—worry and anxiety kill laughter" (p. 211), and suggests that laughter may, in turn, reduce feelings of stress.

30 Don't assume that if there are no complaints, everything is great. Fraser (1986; 1994; 2000) notes that teachers tend to think the classroom environment is more positive than students do. It's important to seek feedback from students about climate.

Chapter 2

1 Curriculum guide objectives tend to be vague because they are produced by a committee and reviewed and amended by an even bigger committee. To get approved, the statements go from specific, concrete goals to vague and useless generalities because that's what committees can agree on. The prevalence of such statements in curriculum guides and other educational literature probably accounts, in part, for the failure of teachers to write, or even think seriously about, instructional objectives.

[2] Grolund (1985) recommends starting with words such as *know, understand,* and *appreciate,* and then translating these terms into student behavior.

[3] Postman & Weingartner (1973), p. 33. Many people object to focusing on student behavior, but as Postman and Weingartner know, there really is no alternative. We cannot get inside a student's head to see what he or she knows. Even if we could, it would not suffice: What matters in the end is how the student performs. As someone once said, "One who knows, acts knowingly."

[4] Seymour & Seymour (1992), p. 96.

[5] The National Council of Teachers of English, the American Historical Association, and other organizations have, at one time or another, opposed instructional objectives.

[6] The vast majority of questions on teacher-made tests require only the recall of facts. Benjamin Bloom once reported that "over 95% of the items on teacher-made tests require nothing more than the recollection of facts" (quoted in Chance, April 1987).

Chapter 3

[1] If no one imitated the first step, I would unfold the paper and fold it again. However, I have never had to do this. Student see, student do.

[2] Tattersall (2002).

[3] Marx & Marx (1980); Kim et al. (1981). Contrary to the notion that mistakes are good, retention is generally best when the error rate is low (Holland & Porter, 1961).

[4] Feldman (1980); McKinney et al. (1984); Tennyson et al. (1972).

[5] Harris & Rosenthal (1985).

[6] Carver (1973). On the other hand, I recall a college professor who used an electronic device that allowed students to indicate whether he was speaking too fast or too slowly. He could monitor their anonymous feedback at a console. He found that the feedback he got was always, "slow down." No matter how slowly he spoke, no student ever said, "speed up." Hmmm. Do you think the student feedback may have reflected something other than comprehension difficulty?

[7] See, for example, Dineen et al. (1977); Morgan (2006).

[8] Bugelski (1977), p. 29.

[9] Delquadri et al. (1986); Greenwood (1997). For a different kind of tutoring competition, see Pigott et al. (1986).

[10] See, for example, Morgan (2006); Wright & Cleary (2006).

[11] I mentioned the jigsaw method (Aronson et al. 1978) in chapter 1. See also Johnson et al. (1994); Qin et al. (1995); and Slavin (1983; 1994) on cooperative learning.

[12] The fact that two-thirds of teachers experience voice strain (Smith et al., 1997) is one indication that teachers talk too much.

[13] For an excellent discussion of inquiry teaching, see Collins & Stevens (1982). Inquiry teaching is intuitively appealing, but it is best to heed the warning of Kirschner et al. (2006; see note 16 of the Prologue).

[14] Bruner (1961). The methodology of discovery teaching is unclear. The teacher is *not* to tell students the principle or method required to solve a problem. (This is what they are supposed to discover.) But, as Nuthall and Snook (1973) observed, "What the teacher is to do when he is not telling the student is not always agreed on" (p. 61). Again, discovery teaching is intuitively appealing, but a little goes a long way; see Kirschner et al. (2006).

[15] Kittell (1957).

[16] E.g., Guthrie (1967).

[17] Ben-Hur (1998), p. 661.

Chapter 4

1 Cuban (1993).
2 Anderson et al. (1969).
3 Childress (1998), p. 616.
4 Anderson & Faust (1973), p. 227.
5 Travers et al. (1964).
6 Anderson et al. (1969), p. 115.
7 Yes, sports fans, skilled athletes *do* have imaginary practices in which they think about doing back flips, flying leaps, slalom runs, or whatever, but despite the popularity of this practice, it is a poor substitute for the real thing.
8 Gage (1978), p. 59.
9 There *will* be a Barry in your class—I guarantee it.
10 One way of dealing with this problem is to cheat. The students don't know whose name is on the card you've drawn, assuming you've drawn it yourself, so if you've just asked the question, "What is the autumnal equinox?" and the name on the card is Brett, who barely knows the difference between sunshine and rain, you might simply call on another student. The trouble with cheating is that eventually Brett may notice (or someone else may point out to him) that he never gets asked hard questions. And *that* may be more humiliating than not being able to answer a question.
11 See Armendariz & Umbreit (1999); Christle & Schuster (2004); Gardner et al. (1994); Heward et al. (1996); Shabani & Carr (2004).
12 Rowe (1974). DeTure (1979) tried to train teachers to increase wait time but was not very successful.
13 Ben-Hur (1998).
14 Dillon (1981). For an excellent brief discussion of questioning, see Dillon (1983).
15 Kauchak & Eggen (1989).

Chapter 5

1 Sticklers for detail will no doubt object to my language. Technically, the thermostat doesn't tell the furnace how it is performing. In fact, it doesn't tell the furnace anything. It just closes or opens electrical circuits and this turns the furnace on or off. I concede the point. I have anthropomorphized slightly to draw a clear parallel between thermostatic feedback and teacher feedback. I apologize to all the sticklers.
2 You have to be careful about nonverbal feedback, though, especially in classrooms with students from a variety of cultures. In some societies, for example, if you give someone a thumbs-up sign you might get punched out.
3 Thorndike (1927).
4 Hattie & Timperley (2007).
5 Wolfe (1951), p. 1,267.
6 Kauchak & Eggen (1989), p. 85.
7 Hattie (1992), p. 9.
8 The Teaching Game was not my idea. I first saw it used by psychologist Robert Epstein in the 1980s at a conference for managers sponsored by the Cambridge Center for Behavioral Studies. Others had used it long before that to demonstrate the power of feedback.
9 This procedure is called *shaping,* which is defined as the reinforcement of successive approximations of a desired behavior. Applied behavior analysts have used shaping very effectively in the treatment of behavior disorders, most notably in children with mental retardation and autism. Shaping also can be of great benefit in the instruction of ordinary children learning academic or motor skills. It is a way of systematically teaching "little by little."

[10] Despite the clear superiority of positive feedback, most people (including, alas, most teachers) tend to rely more on negative feedback. Probably one reason for this is the widespread belief that "we learn from our mistakes," which implies that we have a moral obligation to bash people every time they miss the mark. But while we can learn from our mistakes, we learn even more from our successes, so that is what we should focus on. For more on this, see chapter 8. As an example of the bias of teachers toward negative feedback and the greater power of positive feedback, see Buzas & Ayllon (1981). Many parents, especially low-income parents, share the bias for negative feedback, as Hart and Risley (1995) showed.

[11] Sadker & Sadker (1985), p. 359.

[12] Keller (1943; 1945).

[13] See also Hattie & Timperley (2007).

[14] Trowbridge & Cason (1932). This finding has been replicated a number of times. See, for example, Fitts & Posner (1967).

[15] Englemann and Carnine (1982) recommend correcting only one type of error at a time.

[16] Elawar & Corno (1985).

[17] For example, see Balcazar et al. (1986). Komaki and colleagues (1989) found that sailboat captains who gave frequent feedback to crew members, praising them when they performed well and correcting them when they didn't, won more races than captains who didn't give much feedback. Too much feedback can, however, slow learning if it disrupts performance.

[18] Anderson et al. (1979); Black & Williams (1997).

[19] Sadker & Sadker (1985).

[20] Stevenson (1992) notes that in a comparison of elementary students in Chicago, Taipei (Taiwan), and Sendai (Japan), nearly half of the Chicago teachers provided *no* feedback to students when they were engaged in seat work. This seldom happened in Taiwan and almost never happened in Japan. See also Stevenson & Stigler (1994).

[21] Sadker & Sadker (1985).

Chapter 6

[1] It may occur to you, having just read the chapter on feedback, that David might have learned a lot faster if he had gotten some feedback from his instructor, Captain Uuno. The only feedback he got initially was from the simulator itself, which conveyed to him in a harsh way that he was doing something wrong, but not what he could do to improve. Later, a fellow cadet watched David practice and gave him helpful suggestions based on his performance. Similarly, Jonathan Seagull (see the overline quote) might not have needed quite so much practice if Sullivan had provided more feedback along the way. Real simulators can be, by the way, an excellent way to practice; see, for example, Dillon (2006); Barrett et al. (2006).

[2] Those who oppose practice evidently favor the saying, "If at first you don't succeed, skydiving is not for you." The legendary John Wooden, the long-time and highly successful coach of the UCLA basketball team, said that there are eight laws of teaching: explanation, demonstration, imitation, repetition, repetition, repetition, repetition, and repetition. Childress (1998) notes that in sports, repetition is considered honorable, but in academic areas students are always moving on to something new "with not much opportunity to do things a second time and get better" (p. 617).

[3] Bloom (1985; 1986); Ericsson (1991; 1996; 2005); Ericsson et al. (2006). See also Bereiter & Scardamalia (1993); Samuels (2002). Ericsson & Charness (1995) and Howe et al. (1998) even raise the possibility that innate talent is a myth. Halpern and Wai (2007) found that competitive *Scrabble®* players spend an average of 4.5 hours a week memorizing words from the official *Scrabble®* dictionary.

[4] Ericsson (1991; 1996) found that outstanding performance is seldom achieved in less than ten years. The experts Bloom (1985; 1986) studied (among the top 25 in the United States in their fields) required at least a dozen years, and the average was sixteen years. See also Bereiter & Scardamalia (1993).

[5] Barrett et al. (2006).

[6] Bahrick (1984). See also Bahrick & Phelps (1987). Bahrick's tests cover both simple recall items and those that require the application of principles. Interestingly, the amount of forgetting was *not* predicted by student ability as measured by SAT scores.

[7] Bahrick (1993), p. 66. See also Bahrick (2000; 2005). There seem to be two main ways for learning to get into permastore. One is strong emotion. We are genetically programmed to recall vividly the bear that chased us up a tree or the teacher who humiliated us. The other is practice. We are programmed to remember the area where we harvest blackberries every spring (while keeping an eye out for bears), and the Pledge of Allegiance that we recited every morning in school.

[8] See, for example, Conway et al. (1991; 1992).

[9] Gentile (2000) defines transfer as "the ability to use previously learned skills or knowledges in settings or on problems different from the original learning, including the capacity to distinguish when and where those learnings are appropriate" (p. 13).

[10] Gentile (2000). It is surprising how little spontaneous transfer occurs. For example, if you have students practice spelling a word by writing it several times, they might not spell it correctly if you then ask them to type it. For more on transfer, see Ellis (1965), a classic on the subject; and McKeough et al. (1995).

[11] Gentile (2000), p. 15.

[12] Lindsley (1943).

[13] Once again, the stubborn error effect rears its head; see chapter 5. However, I am not willing to say that uninformed practice has no benefit. Once you can perform accurately, additional practice, even without feedback, seems to build smooth, automatic performance. Anyone who has practiced reciting a poem has experienced this. The problem is that without at least occasional feedback, errors can creep in and be practiced.

[14] Sindelar et al. (1990); Yurick et al. (2006).

[15] The teacher might have a recipe box on her desk containing 3 × 5 cards, with each card containing a solution to one of the problems in the day's lesson. When a student completes problem #1, he checks his work against card #1.

[16] As noted above, in *Dinotopia* David's instructor, Captain Uuno, never provided feedback. All he said was, "Do it again!" Captain Uuno should have been dismissed.

[17] See Stahl (2004).

[18] Bahrick & Phelps (1987). The value of spaced (or distributed) practice to both learning and recall was first demonstrated by Ebbinghaus (1885) and is now very well established. See, for example, Ausubel & Youssef (1965); Bahrick (1993); Bjork (1979); Caple (1996); Reynolds & Glaser (1964). Kerfoot et al. (2007) showed that spaced practice helps medical students retain what they learn. However, Dempster (1988) points out that the importance of spaced practice has been largely ignored in education. Reviews are a way of practicing, and they, too, should be spaced (Gay, 1973).

[19] Bahrick (1984); Rovee-Collier (1995). Periodic testing improves recall (Thorne, 2000) and can be even more helpful than time spent studying (Roediger & Karpicke, 2006).

[20] The value of overlearning has been known since the nonsense syllable experiments of Hermann Ebbinghaus (1885), but the definitive study was William Krueger's (1929) experiment in which adults learned words. He found, like Ebbinghaus, that the more overlearning, the better the recall.

[21] See Bloom (1985; 1986); and Ericsson (1991; 1996).

[22] There is some evidence that timed practice gets better retention than other forms of practice. Olander et al. (1986), for example, taught college students through timed-practice and tested retention after eight months. These students remembered more than stu-

dents who learned the material in the traditional way. However, Doughty et al. (2004) concluded that rate-building procedures have not been shown to be superior to other forms of practice.

23 People who think that practice can't be fun should spend some time in a video arcade watching kids play Blood Sucking Space Monsters. See Loftus & Loftus (1983).

24 Zeelenberg et al. (2001) suggest that people naturally feel regret when they make errors and want to correct them.

25 Inexpensive software programs, such as Crossword Magic,® make it easy for teachers to construct crossword puzzles.

26 Some people object to competition (Kohn, 1992), but most kids and adults enjoy friendly rivalry, and some psychologists even consider competition a basic human need (Reiss, 2005).

Chapter 7

1 Assigning grades is a part of the teacher's job, but it has little to do with either teaching or assessment so I have banished my thoughts on grades to the back of the book. See Appendix A.

2 Though the idea will seem strange to many, it is not new. See Bloom & Madaus (1981).

3 If you are tempted to look down your nose at students who have not learned much, keep in mind that if they have not learned much, you have not taught much.

4 Some readers will be surprised that there is no discussion here of so-called "authentic" forms of assessment (Popham, 2002). Authentic assessment refers to having students do "real world" things to demonstrate what they have learned. A home economics student might, for example, prepare a menu and this would be used to evaluate her writing skill. While such exercises are undoubtedly useful *learning* activities, they lack precision as assessments. Their popularity seems to stem from the current hostility of educators toward tests. There is also no discussion here of portfolios. These are folders in which the student keeps a file of his work, usually his best work. (The shabby stuff is discarded.) As Joan Smutny (2003) writes, "The primary focus of portfolios is on students' strengths . . ." (p. 40). Portfolios are not about assessment. They are about good feelings. They are based on the unsupported beliefs that (1) having a folder full of good work will raise self-esteem, and (2) improved self-esteem results in more learning. Since portfolios are not assessment tools, there is no place for them in a chapter on assessment.

5 Fluency was discussed in chapter 6.

6 The correct answer is b, Carl Rogers.

7 Paine (1776). The correct order is 3-2-1-4. I have changed the punctuation a bit to render it more suitable for my illustration. My apologies to Mr. Paine. (He has been dead a long time and probably won't mind.)

8 B. F. Skinner (1958) pointed out this flaw in multiple choice items long ago.

9 See chapters 3 and 6. The stubborn error effect probably occurs any time students give wrong answers, whether in writing an essay, answering a question in class, or exchanging ideas with students. However, multiple choice items may be particularly prone to this problem. For this reason, it is especially important to provide feedback about multiple choices items as soon as possible after the students answer them. The ideal way to do that is to have students take tests using computer software that records the students' answers and then immediately provides feedback.

10 See, for example, Mawhinney et al. (1971); Kulik & Kulik (1979).

11 See Kaplan & Owings (2002). Testing is often regarded by teachers as a drain on instructional time, but periodic testing actually improves learning and recall (Roediger & Karpicke, 2006; Thorne, 2000).

Chapter 8

[1] I had been had: The teacher invited me to speak merely to save herself the trouble of preparing a lesson.

[2] This is like a doctor saying, "I'll practice medicine, but don't ask me to treat sick people." In my view, teachers who think this way should find another line of work. Motivating students is part of teaching.

[3] Saying this does not mean that biology plays no part in motivation. Illness (including some chronic medical disorders that are not easily recognized), certain prescription drugs, use of alcohol and other psychoactive drugs, and lack of sleep can affect motivation. But most of the time, a lack of student motivation has to do with things that go on—or don't go on—in the classroom.

[4] There is not much dispute about the idea that failure and threats of punishment are demotivating. See, for example, Deci & Cascio (1972).

[5] Some will argue that there are students who simply don't care about succeeding at school tasks, or anything else. But I think the poet Emily Dickinson came closer to the mark when she wrote, "Success is counted sweetest/By those who ne'er succeed." The problem is to arrange things so that students *can* succeed.

[6] There is a note of hypocrisy in opposition to rewards—somehow they are bad for the kids, but good for the grown-ups. As social psychologist Albert Bandura (1986) observed, "Social commentators who decry the use of extrinsic incentives rarely forswear such rewards for themselves when it comes to salary increases, book royalties, and performance fees, for fear the currency of the realm will sap their interest. Valued rewards are accepted as though innocuous to oneself but harmful to others" (p. 250).

[7] The distinction is made between intrinsic rewards (those arising from the behavior itself—the pleasure from eating ice cream, for example) and extrinsic rewards (those provided by others, such as money or praise for eating broccoli). Though widely accepted, the distinction is problematic. For instance, if you read a joke and it makes you laugh, the humor seems to be an intrinsic reward for reading jokes. But suppose you tell someone the joke and she laughs. Is *her* laughter an intrinsic reward or an extrinsic reward? The person's laughter is the natural result of hearing the joke, so it seems to be intrinsic; but it came from another person, not the joke itself, so it seems extrinsic. (If you tell a joke in a room by yourself, you won't hear anyone laugh.) For a discussion of this topic, see Bandura (1986) and Reiss (2005).

[8] See Dickinson (1989).

[9] One wonders whether this principal praises his teachers when they do well. Does he think praising teachers for good work will reduce their interest in teaching? An *Industry Week* poll found that 63% of workers say they do not enjoy their job (Poe & Courter, 1991). Fewer than 10% complain of low pay. A third complain of the lack of praise. Is there reason to believe that workers, including teachers, need praise, but students do not?

[10] For recent reviews and analysis, pro and con, see Akin-Little et al. (2004); Cameron & Pierce (2002); Cameron et al. (2001); Deci et al. (2001); and Henderlong & Lepper (2002).

[11] Lepper et al. (1973).

[12] Others have found the same thing, e.g., Amabile et al. (1986). As Cameron and Pierce (2002) point out, what this actually demonstrates is that *promises* of reward are detrimental, not that rewards are.

[13] Kohn (1993), p. 69. Notice that Kohn's book title includes the phrase "and Other Bribes." The title suggests that praise and awards for achievements constitute bribes. (By the same standard, the teacher's salary and Kohn's book royalties are also bribes.) But the dictionaries I consulted do not equate rewards with bribes. A bribe is defined as something that is offered in advance for committing an illegal, immoral, or unethical act. A reward, by contrast, is something of value given in recognition of an achievement. The

lobbyist who offers a legislator money in exchange for a vote is attempting to bribe him. The teacher who offers to give a student a certificate for achieving a high standard in reading is not bribing him. It is an embarrassment to education that so many educators have failed to see this fundamental difference.

14 You might think I am forgetting Alfie Kohn, who has little if anything good to say about rewards. But Kohn is an education writer, not a researcher. Most of the negative research findings have come from social psychologists (in particular Teresa Amabile, Edward Deci, Richard Ryan, Mark Lepper, and David Greene), but there are also critics of reward among educational researchers, cognitive psychologists, and behavior analysts. You might be surprised to learn that some behavior analysts have criticized the educational use of rewards, but it's true. B. F. Skinner (1968) suggested that with healthy children, success and the "natural rewards" of the activity are usually sufficient. Skinner collaborator Charles Ferster (1967) took a similar view. More recently, behavior analyst Michael Perone (2003) has been harsh (though not Kohnian harsh) in his criticism of rewards. On the other hand, the educational researcher Benjamin Bloom (1976) and social psychologist Albert Bandura (1986), both prominent figures in their field and neither of them a "Skinnerian," *support* the use of extrinsic rewards.

15 Childress (1998), p. 617.

16 Vasta & Stirpe (1979).

17 Mawhinney (1990). See also, for example, Feingold & Mahoney (1975), Mawhinney (1992), Mawhinney et al. (1989), and the various reviews and meta-analyses cited in note 10. Reiss (2005) notes that "almost nobody" who participated in studies on the effect of reward has actually said that the rewards made them feel less interested in the activity. Makes you wonder, doesn't it?

18 Hotard & Cortez (1987).

19 See also the study by McNinch et al. (1995) on the Earning by Learning program, in which at-risk students received $2 for each book they read.

20 Greene & Lepper (1974, p. 54). They continue, "Similarly, if a child does not possess the basic skills to discover the intrinsic satisfactions of complex activities such as reading, the use of extrinsic rewards may be required to equip him with these skills. Finally, if rewards provide him with new information about his ability at a particular task, this may bolster his feelings of competence and his desire to engage in that task for its own sake" (p. 54). Remember, this support for the use of rewards comes from two of the strongest *critics* of reward.

21 Vasta & Stirpe (1979).

22 Deci (1972, p. 58; emphasis added). Also see Deci & Cascio (1972); Ryan et al. (1983, p. 737). For more on the effective use of praise, see Brophy (1981).

23 Bandura (1986, p. 241).

24 Kohn (1993, p. 73); see also his article in *Education Week* (Kohn, 1995). I'm not a big fan of food rewards, partly because most American kids already get more calories than they need. But pizzas are not the only (or even the main) reward provided in the BookIt! program. Students can earn a variety of rewards, including shoelaces, pencil sharpeners, pens, and pencils, none of which provide any calories.

25 Institute of Human Science and Services of the University of Rhode Island (1986).

26 Flora & Flora (1999).

27 In a separate study, Flora and Poponak (2004) compared college students who had been paid for getting good grades as they were growing up with those who had not. Both groups (91% of those paid and 87% of those not paid) said they enjoyed college. However, those who had been paid for grades had significantly higher GPAs—3.29 vs. 2.88. Whether the payments for grades actually increased interest in academics is uncertain, but it certainly didn't do any harm.

28 Quoted in Murray (1997), p. 26.

29 See Cameron & Pierce (1994); Deci & Cascio (1972). After a review of the literature, Morgan (1984) wrote, "The evidence seems to support strongly the hypothesis that

rewards that emphasize success or competence on a task enhance intrinsic motivation" (p. 9).

30 My favorite silly prize, one to be offered only for a significant achievement, is a forty-foot yacht. This is a toy cabin cruiser about a foot long. Attached to each side are twenty tiny plastic feet—a forty-foot yacht! Is that funny, or what?

31 See also Amabile et al. (1986). Recent research suggests that unexpected rewards stimulate the release of dopamine—one of the brain's "intrinsic" rewards. See Blakeslee (2002); Johnson (2005).

32 For more on Lang's program visit www.ihad.org. For a proposal concerning extending the Lang program, see Richmond (1990). For more on Project Choice, see Gibson (1991).

33 Heller et al. (1982), p. 81.

34 See, for example, Rosenfield et al. (1980).

35 Quoted in Murray (1997), p. 26.

36 See Morine-Dershimer (1982) on the negative effects of *undeserved* praise. The self-esteem fad was based on the premise that raising self-esteem would increase motivation and improve learning, and that the way to raise self-esteem was to lavish praise on students, regardless of their achievements. I know of no good evidence to support these ideas (Baumeister et al., 1996; Baumeister, 1999). Fortunately, the self-esteem fad seems to be "losing esteem" (Adler, 1992; Sarler, 1992).

37 Sulzer-Azaroff & Mayer (1977); Brophy (1981).

38 Mueller & Dweck (1998).

39 Quoted in Daviss (2003), p. 37.

40 It is ironic that educators associate Skinner with extrinsic rewards, when in fact he emphasized "natural" rewards (rewards not provided by the teacher) in education. (See his book, *The Technology of Teaching*.) In his teaching machines, the precursor to today's educational software, the only reward for answering correctly was the opportunity to proceed to the next problem. Some instructional software programs today operate on the same principle.

Chapter 9

1 Belmont & Butterfield (1971).

2 Notice that the learning gap would not shrink because we are reducing the learning rate of the faster students, but because we are *increasing* the learning rate of the slower students.

3 I reviewed a number of these programs in *Thinking in the Classroom: A Survey of Programs* (Chance, 1986). Philosophy for Children, for example, is a program that focuses on developing critical thinking skills. See Perkins & Grotzer (1997) for more on teaching thinking skills.

4 The value of spaced practice was pointed out in chapter 6. See Stahl et al. (2004).

5 Pterodactyls get their name from the fact that their wings consisted of a flap of skin that extended from a very long finger to their body.

6 See Chance (1981); Feuerstein (1980). Feuerstein worked with neglected children with low IQs. He referred to them as "retarded performers" because although they functioned as though retarded, he believed many had, as a result of deficient environments, failed to learn the cognitive skills required for normal intelligence.

7 Meichenbaum & Goodman (1971), p. 117.

8 It is often suggested that the problem solver's "unconscious mind" is working on the problem during these "incubation periods," as they are called. But there is a simpler, more elegant explanation: forgetting (Fraley, 2005; Woodworth, 1938). When we set a problem aside, we forget, to some extent, the old, failed approaches and are therefore more likely to see things that had initially escaped our attention.

Chapter 10

[1] Frank McCourt, the retired teacher and Pulitzer-Prize-winning author of *Angela's Ashes*, wrote about his years as a New York City high school teacher in his book, *Teacher Man* (2005).

[2] McCourt (2005), p. 16.

[3] McCourt (2005), p. 16. McCourt reports that he was later reprimanded by the school principal, who was observing from outside the room, for eating lunch in front of his students.

[4] Langdon (1997). More recent surveys have produced similar results. See Public Agenda (May, 2004) and "Parents, teachers agree . . ." (2006).

[5] As always, teacher and student names have been changed to avoid embarrassing people, including those who deserve to be embarrassed.

[6] Patterson & Gullion (1968).

[7] Smith (1985).

[8] Wink (1996) met with high school students in focus groups. She writes, "According to these students, what their schools most lack—and what students most want—are discipline and order" (p. 12). Similarly, Latham (1997) reports that "Students generally feel that school is (1) too easy and (2) too permissive."

[9] Kounin (1970) made a similar point long ago, and Smith (1985) went so far as to write that "teachers are the architects of classroom disorder" (p. 686). Of course, teachers are also the architects of classroom *order*.

[10] The term seems to be equivalent to the term "behavioral momentum," first proposed by John Nevin (Mace et al., 1992). It refers to the tendency to continue in an activity despite a lack of success or other rewards or even in the face of repeated disappointments. The concept was apparently first suggested by sportscasters, who often make statements such as, "The Turtles now have the momentum!"

[11] McCord (1945).

[12] Collins & Tamarkin (1982), p. 182.

[13] Numerous experiments have shown that attending to appropriate student behavior results in fewer disruptions. See Ayllon et al. (1972); Beaman & Wheldall (2000); Deitz & Repp (1983); Elliot & Busse (1991); Hall et al. (1968); Hart et al. (1964); McNamara (1987); Repp et al. (1991).

[14] Thomas et al. (1968).

[15] Madsen et al. (1968). If you're using Latham's Rule of Eight (see chapter 1), you're probably noticing the good stuff. Becker et al. (1971) recommended that teachers use the misbehavior of one child as a signal to praise the appropriate analogous behavior of another child. For example, if Randolph wanders away from his desk when he should be doing seat work, tell Alice that you appreciate the fact that she is in her "office" and hard at work.

[16] Dickinson (1974). Token economies can produce powerful results (see, for example, Staats & Butterfield, 1965). However, they require some thought and planning (see Appendix C).

[17] See, for example, Anderson & Kincaid (2005).

[18] See, for example, O'Leary et al. (1970).

[19] Smith (1985) p. 687.

[20] See, for example, Abramowitz et al. (1987); Madsen et al. (1970); O'Leary et al. (1970); Piazza et al. (1999).

[21] Taylor & O'Reilly (1997).

[22] Figures are from www.stophitting.com/disatschool/statesBanning.php. For more on this topic, see Lyman (2006).

[23] Other forms of punishment can also have adverse effects, but they generally tend to be milder. For more on corporal punishment, visit the Web site of the National Center for the Study of Corporal Punishment and Alternatives (www.temple.edu/education/pse/

NCSCPA.html). For a thorough discussion of the adverse effects of punishment by an expert, see Sidman (2000).

[24] As the child is moved back and forth, the brain also moves. When the child is pulled forward, the brain is forced against the *back* of the skull; when the child is pushed backward, the brain hits the *front* of the skull. Cerebrospinal fluid surrounds the brain and provides a cushion against these impacts, but the brain can still be bruised and blood vessels ruptured. Permanent brain damage and death can occur, especially when babies and small children are shaken.

[25] Sidman (2000).

Epilogue

[1] This parable is not of my invention. I heard or read it somewhere, perhaps in the context of environmental protection, but I don't recall where, so I cannot acknowledge the source. I offer my apology to its originator.

Appendix B

[1] Keller, F. S., & Sherman, J. G. (1982). *The PSI handbook: Essays on personalized instruction.* Lawrence, KS: TRI Publications.

References

Abramowitz, A. J., O'Leary, S. G., & Rosen, L. A. (1987). Reducing off-task behavior in the classroom: A comparison of encouragement and reprimands. *Journal of Abnormal and Clinical Psychology, 15,* 153–163.

Adler, J. (1992, February 17) Hey, I'm terrific! *Newsweek,* pp. 46–51.

Akin-Little, K., Eckert, T. L., Lovett, B. J., & Little, S. G. (2004). Extrinsic reinforcement in the classroom: Bribery or best practice. *School Psychology Review, 33,* 344–362.

Amabile, T. (1989, October). Cashing in on good grades. *Psychology Today,* 80.

Amabile, T. M., Hennessey, B. A., & Grossman, B. S. (1986). Social influences on creativity: The effects of contracted-for reward. *Journal of Personality and Social Psychology, 50*(1), 14–23.

Anderson, C. M., & Kincaid, D. (2005). Applying behavior analysis to school violence and discipline problems: School wide positive behavioral support. *The Behavior Analyst, 28,* 49–63.

Anderson, L., Evertson, C., & Brophy, J. (1979). An experimental study of effective teaching in first grade reading groups. *Elementary School Journal, 79,* 193–223.

Anderson, R. C., & Faust, G. W. (1973). *Educational psychology: The science of instruction and learning.* New York: Dodd, Mead.

Anderson, R. C., Faust, G. W., Roderick, M. C., Cunningham, D. J., & Andre, T. (Eds.). (1969). *Current research on instruction.* Englewood Cliffs, NJ: Prentice-Hall.

Armendariz, F., & Umbreit, J. (1999). Using active response cards to reduce disruptive behavior in a general education classroom. *Journal of Positive Behavioral Interventions, 1,* 152–158.

Aronson, E. (2000). *Nobody left to hate.* San Francisco: Freeman.

Aronson, E., Blaney, N., Stephan, C., Sikes, J., & Snapp, M. (1978). *The jigsaw classroom.* Beverly Hills, CA: Sage.

Aronson, E., & Patnoe, S. (1997). *The jigsaw classroom: Building cooperation in the classroom* (2nd ed.). New York: Longman.

Ausubel, D. P., & Youssef, M. (1965). The effects of spaced repetition on meaningful retention. *Journal of General Psychology, 73,* 147–150.

Ayllon, T., Layman, D., & Burke, S. (1972). Disruptive behavior and reinforcement of academic performance. *Psychological Record, 22,* 315–323.

Ayllon, T., & Roberts, M. D. (1974). Eliminating discipline problems by strengthening academic performance. *Journal of Applied Behavior Analysis, 7,* 71–76.

Bahrick, H. P. (1984). Semantic memory content in permastore: Fifty years of memory for Spanish learned in school. *Journal of Experimental Psychology: General, 113*, 1–29.

Bahrick, H. P. (1993). Extending the lifetime of knowledge. In L. A. Penner, G. M. Batsche, H. M. Knoff, & D. L. Nelson (Eds.), *The challenge in mathematics and science education: Psychology's response* (pp. 61–82). Washington, DC: American Psychological Association.

Bahrick, H. P. (2000). Long-term maintenance of knowledge. In E. Tulving & F. I. M. Craik (Eds.), *The Oxford handbook of memory* (pp. 347–362). New York: Oxford University Press.

Bahrick, H. P. (2005). The long-term neglect of long-term memory: Reasons and remedies. In A. F. Healy (Ed.), *Experimental cognitive psychology and its applications* (pp. 89–100). Washington, DC: American Psychological Association.

Bahrick, H. P., & Phelps, E. (1987). Retention of Spanish vocabulary over 8 years. *Journal of Experimental Psychology: Learning, Memory, and Cognition, 13*, 344–349.

Balcazar, F., Hopkins, B. L., & Suarez, Y. (1986). A critical, objective review of performance feedback. *Journal of Organizational Behavior Management, 7*, 65–89.

Bandura, A. (1986). *Social foundations of thought and action: A social cognitive theory.* Upper Saddle River, NJ: Prentice Hall.

Banner, J. M., Jr., & Cannon, H. C. (1997). *The elements of teaching.* New Haven, CT: Yale University Press.

Banner, J. M., Jr., & Cannon, H. C. (1997, April). The pleasure principle. *Teacher Magazine*, pp. 44–45.

Barr, R., & Dreeben, R. (1983). *How schools work.* Chicago: University of Chicago Press.

Barrett, M. J., Kuzman, M. A., Seto, T. C., Richards, P., Mason, D., Barrett, C. M., & Gracely, E. J. (2006). The power of repetition in mastering cardiac auscultation. *American Journal of Medicine, 119*, 73–75.

Baumeister, R. F. (1999, January). Low self-esteem does not cause aggression. *APA Monitor, 7.*

Baumeister, R. F., Smart, L., & Boden, J. M. (1996). Relation of threatened egotism to violence and aggression: The dark side of high self-esteem. *Psychological Review, 103*, 5–33.

Beaman, R., & Wheldall, K. (2000). Teachers' use of approval and disapproval in the classroom. *Educational Psychology, 20*, 431–446.

Becker, W., Engelmann, S., & Thomas, D. R. (1971). *Teaching: A course in applied psychology.* Chicago: Science Research Associates.

Belmont, J. M., & Butterfield, E. C. (1971). Learning strategies as determinants of memory deficiencies. *Cognitive Psychology, 2*, 411–420.

Ben-Hur, M. (1998, May). Mediation of cognitive competencies for students in need. *Phi Delta Kappan*, 661–666.

Bereiter, C., & Scardamalia, M. (1993). *Surpassing ourselves: An inquiry into the nature and implications of expertise.* Chicago: Open Court.

Berg, S. (1998, January 21). Report card for teachers: Can computers measure the art of teaching. *Star Tribune* (TN). Retrieved from http://www.shearonforschools.com/news_star_tribune_12198.htm

Bjork, R. A. (1979). Improving processing analysis of college teaching. *Educational Psychology, 14*, 15–23.

Black, P., & Williams, D. (1997). Assessment and classroom learning. *Assessment in Education, 5*, 1–89.

Blakeslee, S. (2002, February 19). Highjacking the brain circuits with a nickel slot machine. *The New York Times.* Retrieved from http://www.nytimes.com/2002/02/19/health/19REWA.html?ex=1015483708&ei=1&en=246172b28577ab32.

Bloom, B. (1976). *Human characteristics and school learning.* New York: McGraw-Hill.

Bloom, B. (1985). *Developing talent in young people.* New York: Ballantine.

Bloom, B. (1986, February). Automaticity: "The hands and feet of genius." *Educational Leadership,* 70–77.

Bloom, B., & Madaus, G. (1981). *Evaluation to improve learning.* New York: McGraw-Hill.

Bradley, A. (1997, April). Hardly working. *Teacher Magazine,* pp. 20–21.

Bridges, E. M. (1996). Evaluation for tenure and dismissal. In J. Millman & L. Hammond (Eds.), *The new handbook of teacher evaluation* (pp. 147–157). Newberry Park: Sage.

Brophy, J. (1981). Teacher praise: A functional analysis. *Review of Educational Research, 51,* 5–32.

Brophy, J., & Good, T. (1970). Teachers' communication of differential expectations for children's classroom performances: Some behavioral data. *Journal of Educational Psychology, 61,* 365–374.

Brophy, J., & Good, T. L. (1986). Teacher behavior and student achievement. In M. C. Wittrock (Ed.), *Handbook of research on teaching* (3rd ed., pp. 328–375). New York: Macmillan.

Bruner, J. (1960/1977). *The process of education.* Cambridge, MA: Harvard University Press.

Bruner, J. S. (1961). The act of discovery. *Harvard Education Review, 31,* 21–32.

Bugelski, B. R. (1977). *Some practical laws of learning.* Bloomington, IN: Phi Delta Kappa Foundation.

Buzas, H. P., & Ayllon, T. (1981). Differential reinforcement in coaching tennis skills. *Behavior Modification, 5,* 372–385.

Cameron, J., Banko, K. M., & Pierce, W. D. (2001). Pervasive negative effects of rewards on intrinsic motivation: The myth continues. *The Behavior Analyst, 24,* 1–44.

Cameron, J., & Pierce, W. D. (1994). Reinforcement, reward and intrinsic motivation: A meta-analysis. *Review of Educational Research, 64*(3), 363–423.

Cameron, J., & Pierce, W. D. (1996). The debate about rewards and intrinsic motivation: Protests and accusations do not alter the results. *Review of Educational Research, 66,* 39–51.

Cameron, J., & Pierce, W. D. (2002). *Rewards and intrinsic motivation: Resolving the controversy.* Westport, CT: Bergin & Garvey.

Caple, C. (1996). *The effects of spaced practice and review on recall and retention using computer assisted instruction.* Ann Arbor, MI: UMI.

Carver, R. P. (1973). Effect of increasing the rate of speech presentation upon comprehension. *Journal of Educational Psychology, 65,* 118–126.

Chance, P. (1981, October). The remedial thinker. *Psychology Today,* 63–70.

Chance, P. (1986). *Thinking in the classroom: A survey of programs.* New York: Teachers College Press.

Chance, P. (1987, April). Master of mastery. *Psychology Today,* 43–46.

Chance, P. (1992, November). The rewards of learning. *Phi Delta Kappan,* 200–207.

Chance, P. (1993, June). Sticking up for rewards. *Phi Delta Kappan,* 787–790.

Childress, H. (1998, April). Seventeen reasons why football is better than high school. *Phi Delta Kappan*, 616–619.

Christle, C. A., & Schuster, J. W. (2004). The effects of using response cards on student participation, academic achievement, and on-task behavior during whole-class math instruction. *Journal of Behavioral Education, 12*, 147–165.

Collins, A., & Stevens, A. L. (1982). Goals and strategies of inquiry teachers. In R. Glaser (Ed.), *Advances in instructional psychology* (vol. 2, pp. 65–119). Hillsdale, NJ: Erlbaum.

Collins, M., & Tamarkin, C. (1982). *Marva Collins' way*. Los Angeles: J. P. Tarcher.

Conway, M. A., Cohen, G., & Stanhope, N. (1991). On the very long-term retention of knowledge acquired through formal education: Twelve years of cognitive psychology. *Journal of Experimental Psychology: General, 20*, 395–409.

Conway, M. A., Cohen, G., & Stanhope, N. (1992). Very long-term memory for knowledge acquired at school and university. *Applied Cognitive Psychology, 6*, 467–482.

Cuban, L. (1993). *How teachers taught: Constancy and change in American classrooms, 1890–1990*. New York: Teachers College Press.

Daviss, B. (2003, June). Taking the blade. *America West*, pp. 20–38.

Deci, E. (1971). Effects of externally mediated rewards on intrinsic motivation. *Journal of Personality and Social Psychology, 18*, 105–115.

Deci, E. (1972, August). Work—Who does not like it and why. *Psychology Today*, 56–61, 84, 86–87.

Deci, E. (1975). *Intrinsic motivation*. New York: Plenum.

Deci, E., & Cascio, W. F. (1972, April). *Changes in intrinsic motivation as a function of negative feedback and threats*. Paper presented at the Eastern Psychological Association, Boston, MA.

Deci, E. L., Koestner, R., & Ryan, R. M. (2001). Extrinsic rewards and intrinsic motivation in education: Reconsidered once again. *Review of Educational Research, 71*, 1–27.

Deitz, D. E. D., & Repp, A. C. (1983). Reducing behavior through reinforcement. *Exceptional education Quarterly, 3*, 34–46.

Delquadri, J., Greenwood, D., Carta, J. J., & Hall, R. V. (1986). Classwide peer tutoring. *Exceptional Children, 52*, 535–542.

Dempster, F. N. (1988). The spacing effect: A case study in the failure to apply the results of psychological research. *American Psychologist, 43*, 627–634.

DeTure, L. (1979). Relative effects of modeling on the acquisition of wait-time by preservice elementary teachers and concomitant changes in dialogue patterns. *Journal of Research in Science Teaching, 16*, 553–562.

Dickinson, A. M. (1989). The detrimental effects of extrinsic reinforcement on "intrinsic motivation." *The Behavior Analyst, 12*, 1–15.

Dickinson, D. (1974). But what happens when you take that reinforcement away? *Psychology in the Schools, 11*, 158–160.

Dillon, J. T. (1981). Duration of response to teacher questions and statements. *Contemporary Educational Psychology, 6*, 1–11.

Dillon, J. T. (1983). *Teaching and the art of questioning*. Bloomington, IN: Phi Delta Kappa Educational Foundation.

Dillon, S. (2006, October 20). No test tubes? Debate on virtual science classes. *New York Times*, pp. A1, A20.

Dineen, J. P., Clark, H. B., & Risley, T. R. (1977). Peer tutoring among elementary students: Educational benefits to the tutor. *Journal of Applied Behavior Analysis, 10,* 231–238.

Doughty, S. S., Chase, P. N., & O'Shields, E. M. (2004). Effects of rate building on fluent performance: A review and commentary. *The Behavior Analyst, 27,* 7–23.

Earthman, G. I. (2002). *School facility conditions and student academic achievement.* Los Angeles: UCLA Institute for Democracy, Education and Access (IDEA).

Ebbinghaus, H. (1885). *Memory, a contribution to experimental psychology* (H. A. Ruger, Trans., 1913). New York: Columbia University Press.

Eisenberger, R. (1992). Learned industriousness. *Psychological Review, 99,* 248–267.

Eisenberger, R., & Cameron, J. (1996). The detrimental effects of reward: Myth or reality? *American Psychologist, 51,* 1153–1166.

Eisenberger, R., & Cameron, J. (1998). Rewards, intrinsic interest and creativity: New findings. *American Psychologist, 53,* 676–679.

Eisenberger, R., & Rhoades, L. (2001). Incremental effects of reward on creativity. *Journal of Personality and Social Psychology, 81,* 728–741.

Ekman, P. (2007). *Emotions revealed: Recognizing faces and feelings to improve communication and emotional life.* New York: Owl Books.

Elawar, M. C., & Corno, L. (1985). A factorial experiment in teachers' written feedback on student homework: Changing teacher behavior a little rather than a lot. *Journal of Educational Psychology, 77,* 162–173.

Elliott, S. N., & Busse, R. T. (1991). Social skills assessment with children and adolescents. *School Psychology International, 12,* 63–83.

Ellis, H. C. (1965). *The transfer of learning.* New York: Macmillan.

Engelmann, S., & Carnine, D. (1982). *Theory of instruction: Principles and applications.* New York: Irvington.

Ericsson, K. A. (1991). *Toward a general theory of expertise.* Cambridge, UK: Cambridge University Press.

Ericsson, K. A. (Ed.). (1996). *The road to excellence: The acquisition of expert performance in the arts and sciences, sports and games.* Mahwah, NJ: Erlbaum.

Ericsson, K. A. (2005). Recent advances in expertise research: A commentary on the contribution to the special issue. *Applied Cognitive Psychology, 19,* 223–241.

Ericsson, K. A., & Charness, N. (1994). Expert performance: Its structure and acquisition. *American Psychologist, 48,* 725–747.

Ericsson, K. A., & Charness, N. (1995). Abilities: Evidence for talent or characteristics acquired through engagement in relevant activities? *American Psychologist, 50,* 803–804.

Ericsson, K. A., Charness, N., Feltovich, P. J., & Hoffman, R. R. (2006). *The Cambridge handbook of expertise and expert performance.* Cambridge, UK: Cambridge University Press.

Feingold, B. D., & Mahoney, M. J. (1975). Reinforcement effects on intrinsic interest: Undermining the overjustification hypothesis. *Behavior Therapy, 6,* 367–377.

Feldman, K. V. (1980). The effect of number of positive and negative instances, concept definition, and of mathematical concepts. *Review of Educational Research, 50,* 33–67.

Ferster, C. B. (1967). Arbitrary and natural reinforcement. *Psychological Record, 17,* 341–367.

Feuerstein, R. (1980). *Instrumental enrichment.* New York: University Park Press.

Fitts, P. M., & Posner, M. J. (1967). *Human performance*. Belmont, CA: Brooks/Cole.

Flora, S. R. (1990). Undermining intrinsic interest from the standpoint of a behaviorist. *Psychological Record, 40*, 323–346.

Flora, S. R., & Flora, D. B. (1999). Effects of extrinsic reinforcement for reading during childhood on reported reading habits of college students. *Psychological Record, 49*, 3–14.

Flora, S. R., & Poponak, S. S. (2004). Childhood payment for grades is related to college grade point averages. *Psychological Reports, 94*, 66.

Foreman, J. (2003, August 5). The 43 facial muscles that reveal the most fleeting emotions. *The New York Times*, pp. F5–F8.

Fraley, L. E. (2005). On verbal behavior: The fourth of four parts. *Behaviorology Today, 8*, 3–18.

Fraser, B. J. (1986). *Classroom environment*. London: Croom Helm.

Fraser, B. J. (1994). Research on classroom and school climate. In D. Gabel (Ed.), *Handbook of research on science teaching and learning* (pp. 493–541).

Fraser, B. J. (2000). Instructional environment. In A. E. Kazdin (Ed.), *Encyclopedia of psychology* (vol. 4, pp. 308–311). Washington, DC: American Psychological Association & Oxford University Press.

Gage, N., & Berliner, D. (1984). *Educational psychology* (3rd ed.). Chicago: Rand McNally.

Gage, N. L. (1978). *Four cheers for research on teaching*. ERIC # 178460.

Galloway, C. (1968). *Nonverbal communication: A needed focus*. ERIC abstract # ED025484.

Gardner, R., III, Heward, W. L., & Grossi, T. A. (1994). Effects of response cards on student participation and academic achievement: A systematic replication with inner-city students during whole class science instruction. *Journal of Applied Behavior Analysis, 27*, 63–71.

Gay, I. R. (1973). Temporal position of reviews and its effect on the retention of mathematical rules. *Journal of Educational Psychology, 64*, 171–182.

Gentile, J. R. (2000). Transfer of learning. In A. E. Kazdin (Ed.), *Encyclopedia of psychology* (vol. 5, pp. 13–16). Washington, DC: American Psychological Association & Oxford University Press.

Gibson, C. (1991, May 17). Project Choice. *Good Morning America*, Journal Graphics transcript #1285.

Greene, D., & Lepper, M. R. (1974, September). Intrinsic motivation: How to turn play into work. *Psychology Today*, 49–54.

Greenwood, C. (1997). Classwide peer tutoring. *Behavior and Social Issues, 7*, 53–57.

Grolund, N. (1985). *Stating objectives for classroom instruction* (2nd ed.). New York: Macmillan.

Guthrie, J. T. (1967). Expository instruction versus a discovery method. *Journal of Educational Psychology, 58*, 45–49.

Hall, R. V., Lund, D., & Jackson, D. (1968). Effects of teacher attention on study behavior. *Journal of Applied Behavior Analysis, 1*, 1–12.

Halpern, D. F., & Wai, J. (2007). The world of competitive Scrabble: Novice and expert differences in visuospatial and verbal abilities. *Journal of Experimental Psychology: Applied, 13*, 79–94.

Harris, M. J., & Rosenthal, R. (1985). Mediation of interpersonal expectancy effects: 31 meta-analyses. *Psychological Bulletin, 97*(3), 363–386.

Hart, B. M., Allen, K. E., Buell, J. S., Harris, F. R., & Wolf, M. M. (1964). Effects of social reinforcement on operant crying. *Journal of Experimental Child Psychology, 1*, 145–153.

Hart, B. M., & Risley, T. R. (1995). *Meaningful differences in the everyday experience of young American children.* Baltimore: Paul H. Brookes.

Hattie, J., & Purdie, N. (2000). Instructional treatments In A. E. Kazdin (Ed.), *Encyclopedia of psychology* (vol. 4, pp. 313–315). Washington, DC: American Psychological Association & Oxford University Press.

Hattie, J., & Timperley, H. (2007). The power of feedback. *Review of Educational Research, 77*, 81–112.

Hattie, J. A. (1992). Measuring the effects of schooling. *Australian Journal of Education, 36*, 5–13.

Haycock, K. (1998, Summer). Good teaching matters . . . a lot. *Thinking K–16, 3*–14.

Heaviside, S., Rowand, C., Williams, C., & Farris, E. (1998). *Violence and discipline problems in U.S. public schools: 1996–1997* (NCES 98-030). Washington, DC: U.S. Department of Education National Center for Education Statistics.

Heller, K., Holtzman, W., & Messick, S. (1982). *Placing children in special education: A strategy for equity.* Washington, DC: National Academy Press.

Henderlong, J., & Lepper, M. R. (2002). The effects of praise on children's intrinsic motivation: A review and synthesis. *Psychological Bulletin, 128*, 774–795.

Heward, W. L., Gardner, R., Cavanaugh, R. A., Courson, F. H., Grossi, T. A., & Barbetta, P. M. (1996). Everyone participates in this class: Using response cards to increase active student response. *Teaching Exceptional Children, 28*(2), 4–10.

Holland, J. G., & Porter, D. (1961). The influence of repetition of incorrectly answered items in a teaching-machine program. *Journal of the Experimental Analysis of Behavior, 4*, 305–307.

Hopkins, B. L., & Conard, R. J. (1975). Putting it all together: Superschool. In N. G. Haring & R. L. Schiefelbusch (Eds.), *Teaching special children* (pp. 342–385). New York: McGraw-Hill.

Hotard, S., & Cortez, M. J. (1987, August). *Evaluation of Lafayette parish job training summer remedial program.* Report presented to the Lafayette parish school board and Lafayette parish job training department of Lafayette parish government.

Howe, M. J. A., Davidson, J. W., & Sloboda, J. A. (1998). Innate talents: Reality or myth? *Behavioral and Brain Sciences, 21*, 399–442.

Institute of Human Science and Services of the University of Rhode Island. (1986). *Pizza Hut Inc.'s BookIt! national reading incentive program. Final evaluation report.* Kingston, RI: Author.

Johnson, D. W., Johnson, R. T., & Holubec, E. J. (1994). *Cooperative learning in the classroom.* Alexandria, VA: Association for Supervision and Curriculum Development.

Johnson, K., & Layng, T. V. J. (1992). Breaking the structuralist barrier: Literacy and numeracy with fluency. *American Psychologist, 47*(11), 1475–1490.

Johnson, K., & Layng, T. V. J. (1994). The Morningside model of generative instruction. In R. Gardner, D. M. Sainto, et al. (Eds.), *Behavior analysis in education.* (pp. 173–197). Pacific Grove, CA: Brooks/Cole.

Johnson, K., & Street, E. M. (2004). The Morningside model of generative instruction: An integration of research-based practices. In D. J. Moran & R. W. Malott (Eds.), *Evidenced-based educational methods* (pp. 247–265). San Diego: Elsevier.

Johnson, S. (2005). *Mind wide open*. New York: Scribner.

Jordan, H. R., Mendro, R. L., & Weerasighe, D. (1997, July). *Teacher effects on longitudinal student achievement*. Paper presented at the National Evaluation Institute, Indianapolis, IN.

Jussim, L. (1989). Teacher expectations: Self-fulfilling prophecies, perceptual biases, and accuracy. *Journal of Personality and Social Psychology, 57,* 469–480.

Kaplan, L. S., & Owings, W. A. (2002). *Enhancing teaching quality*. Bloomington, IN: Phi Delta Kappa Education Foundation.

Karpicke, J. D., & Roediger, H. L., III. (2007). Repeated retrieval during learning is the key to long-term retention. *Journal of Memory & Language, 57,* 151–162.

Kauchak, D. P., & Eggen, P. D. (1989). *Learning and teaching: Research-based method*. Boston: Allyn & Bacon.

Keller, F. S. (1943). Studies in international Morse code: I. A new method of teaching code reception. *Journal of Applied Psychology, 27,* 407–415.

Keller, F. S. (1945). *The radio code research project: Final report of project SC-88 OSRD report 5379*. San Antonio, TX: The Psychological Corporation (PBL 12154).

Keller, F. S., & Sherman, J. G. (1982). *The PSI handbook: Essays on personalized instruction*. Lawrence, KS: TRI Publications.

Kerfoot, B. P., DeWolf, W. C., Masser, B. A., et al. (2007). Spaced education improves the retention of clinical knowledge by medical students: A randomized controlled trial. *Medical Education, 41,* 23–31.

Kim, Y. C., Marx, M. H., & Broyles, J. W. (1981). The stubborn-error effect in verbal discrimination learning. *Bulletin of the Psychonomic Society, 18,* 5–8.

Kirschner, P. A., Swells, J., & Clark, R. E. (2006). Why minimalist guidance during instruction does not work: An analysis of the failure of constructivist, discovery, problem-based, experiential, and inquiry-based teaching. *Educational Psychologist, 41,* 75–86.

Kittell, J. E. (1957). An experimental study of the effect of external direction during learning on transfer and retention of principles. *Journal of Educational Psychology, 48,* 391–405.

Knapp, M. L., & Hall, J. A. (2005). *Nonverbal communication in human interaction*. Belmont, CA: Wadsworth.

Kohn, A. (1992). *No contest: The case against competition* (Rev. ed.). Boston: Houghton-Mifflin.

Kohn, A. (1993). *Punished by rewards: The trouble with gold stars, incentive plans, A's, praise, and other bribes*. Boston: Houghton Mifflin.

Kohn, A. (1995, April 19). Newt Gingrich's reading plan: Money is the wrong motivator for kids. *Education Week*, pp. 42, 52.

Komaki, J. L., Desselles, M. L., & Bowman, E. D. (1989). Definitely not a breeze: Extending the operant model of effective supervision to teams. *Journal of Applied Psychology, 74,* 522–529.

Kounin, J. S. (1970). *Discipline and group management in classrooms*. New York: Holt.

Krueger, W. C. F. (1929). The effects of overlearning on retention. *Journal of Experimental Psychology, 12,* 71–78.

Kulik, J. A. & Kulik, C. C. (1979). College teaching. In P. L. Peterson & H. J. Walberg (Eds.), *Research on teaching: Concepts, findings, and implications*. Berkeley: McCutchan.

Kupyers, O. S., & Becker, W. C. (1967). *How to make a token system fail*. Urbana: Office of Instructional Resources, University of Illinois.

Langdon, C. A. (November, 1997). The fourth Phi Delta Kappa poll of teachers' attitudes toward the public schools. *Phi Delta Kappan, 212*–220.

Latham, G. (1992). Interacting with at-risk children: The positive approach. *Principal, 72,* 26–30.

Latham, G. (1997). *Behind the schoolhouse door.* Logan: Utah State University.

Latham, G. (1997, March 7). A preliminary summary of teachers' and administrators' responses to face-to-face queries about compelling problems in education, and what should be done about them. Talk given before a ULRC Consortium meeting, Salt Lake City, Utah.

Lepper, M. R., Greene, D., & Nisbett, R. E. (1973). Undermining children's intrinsic interest with extrinsic reward: A test of the "overjustification" hypothesis. *Journal of Personality and Social Psychology, 28,* 129–137.

Lindsley, D. B. (1943). *Radar operation training: Results of study of SCR-270-271 operators at Drew Field.* OSRD Report 1737, Yerkes Laboratories of Primate Biology (PBL 18367).

Lipsey, M. W., & Wilson, D. B. (1993). The efficacy of psychological, educational, and behavioral treatment: Confirmation from meta-analysis. *American Psychologist, 48,* 1181–1209.

Loftus, E. F., & Loftus, G. R. (1983). *Mind at play: The psychology of video games.* New York: Basic.

Lorge, I. (1930). *Influence of regularly interpolated time intervals on subsequent learning.* New York: Teachers College Press.

Lyman, R. (2006, September 30). In many public schools, the paddle is no relic. *New York Times,* pp. A1, A13.

Mace, F. C., Lalli, J. S., Shea, M. C., & Nevin, J. A. (1992). Behavioral momentum in college basketball. *Journal of Applied Behavior Analysis, 25,* 657–663.

Madsen, C. H., Becker, W. C., & Thomas, D. R. (1968). Rules, praise, and ignoring: Elements of elementary classroom control. *Journal of Applied Behavior Analysis, 1,* 139–150.

Madsen, C. H., Becker, W. C., Thomas, D. R., Koser, L., & Plager, E. (1970). An analysis of the reinforcing effects of "sit down" commands. In R. K. Parker (Ed.), *Readings in educational psychology* (pp. 265–278). Boston: Allyn & Bacon.

Marx, M. H., & Marx, K. (1980). Confirmation of the stubborn error effect in human multiple-choice verbal learning. *Bulletin of the Psychonomic Society, 16,* 477–479.

Mathews, J. (1988). *Escalante: The best teacher in America.* New York: Holt.

Mathews, M. (1992). Gifted students talk about cooperative learning. *Educational Leadership, 50,* 48–50.

Mawhinney, T. C. (1990). Decreasing intrinsic "motivation" with extrinsic rewards: Easier said that done. *Journal of Organizational Behavior Management, 11,* 175–191.

Mawhinney, T. C., Dickinson, A. M., & Taylor, L. A. (1989). The use of concurrent schedules to evaluate the effects of extrinsic rewards on "intrinsic motivation." *Journal of Organizational Behavior Management, 10,* 109–129.

Mawhinney, V. T., Bostow, D. E., Laws, D. R., Blumenfeld, G. T., & Hopkins, B. L. (1971). A comparison of students studying behavior produced by daily, weekly, and three-week testing schedules. *Journal of Applied Behavior Analysis, 4,* 257–264.

Mayer, G. R. (1995). Preventing antisocial behavior in the schools. *Journal of Applied Behavior Analysis, 28*, 467–478.

McCord, D. (1945). *What cheer: An anthology of American and British humorous and witty verse*. New York: Cowan-McCann.

McCourt, F. (2005). *Teacher man: A memoir*. New York: Scribner.

McKeough, A., Lupart, J., & Marine, A. (Eds.). (1995). *Teaching for transfer*. Mahwah, NJ: Erlbaum.

McKinney, C. W., & Larkin, A. G. (1982). Effects of high, normal, and low teacher enthusiasm on secondary social studies achievement. *Social Education, 46*, 290–292.

McKinney, C. W., Larkin, A. G., & Burts, D. C. (1984). Effects of overt teacher enthusiasm on first grade students' acquisition of three concepts. *Theory and Research in Special Education, 11*, 15–24.

McNamara, E. (1987). Behavioral approaches in the secondary school. In K. Wheldall (Ed.), *The behaviorist in the classroom* (pp. 50–68). London: Allen & Unwin.

McNinch, G. W., Steely, M., & Davidson, T. J. (1995). *Evaluating the earning by learning program: Changing attitudes in reading*. Paper presented at the annual meeting of the Georgia Council of the International Reading Association, Atlanta, GA.

Meichenbaum, D., & Goodman, J. (1971). Training impulsive children to talk to themselves: A means of developing self-control. *Journal of Abnormal Psychology, 77*, 115–126.

Mendel, M. J., & Heath, G. (2004). *A summary of scientific findings on adverse effects of indoor environments on students' health, academic performance and attendance*. Washington, DC: U.S. Department of Education.

Merton, R. K. (1948). The self-fulfilling prophecy. *Antioch Review, 8*, 193–210.

Mobbs, D., Greleus, E. A., Menon, V., & Reiss, A. L. (2003). Humor modulates the inesolimbic reward centers. *Neuron, 40*, 1041–1048.

Morgan, M. (1984). Reward-induced decrements and increments in intrinsic motivation. *Review of Educational Research, 54*(1), 5–30.

Morgan, S. A. (2006). Introduction: Four classwide peer tutoring programs—Research, recommendations for implementation, and future directions. *Reading and Writing Quarterly: Overcoming Learning Difficulties, 22*, 1–4.

Morine-Dershimer, G. (1982). Pupil perception of teacher praise. *Elementary School Journal, 82*, 421–434.

Mueller, C., & Dweck, C. (1998). Praise for intelligence can undermine children's motivation and performance. *Journal of Personality and Social Psychology, 75*(1), 33–52.

Murray, B. (1997, June). Rewards should be given when defined goals are met. *APA Monitor*, p. 26.

Nevin, J. A. (1992). An integrative model for the study of behavioral momentum. *Journal of the Experimental Analysis of Behavior, 57*(3), 301–316.

Nuttall, G., & Snook, J. (1973). Contemporary models of teaching. In R. M. W. Travers (Ed.), *Second Handbook of Research on Teaching* (pp. 47–76). Chicago: Rand McNally.

O'Hair, M. J., & Ropo, E. (1994). Unspoken messages: Understanding diversity in education requires emphasis on nonverbal communication. *Teacher Education Quarterly, 21*, 91–112.

O'Leary, K. D., Kaufman, K. F., Kass, R. E., & Drabman, R. S. (1970). The effects of loud and soft reprimands on the behavior of disruptive students. *Exceptional Children, 37,* 145–155.

Olander, C. P., Collins, D. L., McArthur, B. L., Watts, R. O., & McDade, C. E. (1986). Retention among college students: A comparison of traditional versus precision teaching. *Journal of Precision Teaching, 6,* 80–82.

Paine, T. (1776/1961). The American crisis. In S. Bradley, R. C. Beatty, & E. H. Long (Eds.), *The American tradition in literature* (vol. 1, rev., pp. 260–267). New York: Norton.

Parents, teachers agree—Good educators are key. (2006, February 9). *The (Wilmington) News Journal,* pp. A1, A13.

Patrick, B. C., Hisley, J., & Kempler, T. (2000). "What's everybody so excited about?": The effects of teacher enthusiasm on student intrinsic motivation and vitality. *Journal of Experimental Education, 68,* 217–236.

Patterson, G. R., & Gullion, M. E. (1968). *Living with children: New methods for parents and teachers.* Chicago: Research Press.

Perkins, D. N., & Grotzer, T. A. (1997). Teaching intelligence. *American Psychologist, 52*(10), 1125–1133.

Perone, M. (2003). Negative effects of positive reinforcement. *The Behavior Analyst, 26,* 1–14.

Phillips, P. A., & Smith, L. R. (1992). *The effects of teacher dress on student perception.* ERIC abstract #ED347151.

Piazza, C. C., Bowman, L. G., Centrucci, S. A., Delia, M. D., Adelinis, J. O., & Goh, H. (1999). An evaluation of the properties of attention as reinforcement for destructive and appropriate behavior. *Journal of Applied Behavior Analysis, 32,* 437–449.

Pigott, H. E., Fantuzzo, J. W., & Clement, P. W. (1986). The effect of reciprocal peer tutoring and group contingencies on the academic performance of elementary school children. *Journal of Applied Behavior Analysis, 19,* 93–98.

Poe, R., & Courter, C. L. (1991, September). Fast forward. *Across the Board,* p. 5.

Popham, W. J. (2002). *Classroom assessment: What teachers need to know* (3rd ed.). Boston: Allyn & Bacon.

Postman, N., & Weingartner, C. (1973). *How to recognize a good school.* Bloomington, IN: Phi Delta Kappa.

Provine, R. R. (2000). *Laughter: A scientific investigation.* New York: Viking.

Public Agenda. (2004, May). *Teaching interrupted: Do discipline policies in today's public schools foster the common good?* Retrieved from http://www.publicagenda.org

Qin, Z., Johnson, D. W., & Johnson, R. T. (1995). Cooperative versus competitive efforts and problem solving. *Review of Educational Research, 65,* 129–143.

Ravitch, D. (2001). *Left back: A century of battles over school reform.* New York: Touchstone.

Reiss, S. (2005). Extrinsic and intrinsic motivation at 30: Unresolved scientific issues. *The Behavior Analyst, 28,* 1–14.

Repp, A., Felce, D., & Barton, L. (1991). The effects of initial interval size on the efficacy of DRO schedules of reinforcement. *Exceptional Children, 58,* 417–425.

Reynolds, J. H., & Glaser, R. (1964). Effects of repetition and spaced review upon retention of a complex learning task. *Journal of Educational Psychology, 55,* 297–308.

Richmond, G. (1990, November). The student incentive plan: Mitigating the legacy of poverty. *Phi Delta Kappan, 227*–229.

Roediger, H. L., III, & Karpicke, J. D. (2006). Test-enhanced learning: Taking memory tests improves long-term retention. *Psychological Science, 17,* 249–255.

Rosenfield, D., Folger, R., & Adelman, H. F. (1980). When rewards reflect competence: A qualification of the overjustification effect. *Journal of Personality and Social Psychology, 39*(3), 368–376.

Rosenshine, B. V. (1986, April). Synthesis of research on explicit teaching. *Educational Leadership,* 60–69.

Rosenshine, B. V., & Stevens, R. J. (1986). Teaching functions. In M. D. Wittrock (Ed.), *The handbook of research on teaching* (3rd ed.). New York: Macmillan.

Rosenthal, R. (1973, September). The Pygmalion effect lives. *Psychology Today,* 56–63.

Rosenthal, R. (1995). Critiquing Pygmalion: A 25-year perspective. *Current Directions in Psychological Science, 6*(6), 169–172.

Rosenthal, R. (2002). Covert communication in classrooms, clinics, courtrooms, and cubicles. *American Psychologist, 57,* 839–849.

Rosenthal, R., Archer, D., DiMatteo, M. R., Koivumaki, J. H., & Rogers, P. L. (1974, September). Body talk and tone of voice: The language without words. *Psychology Today,* 64–68.

Rosenthal, R., & Jacobson, L. (1968). *Pygmalion in the classroom: Teacher expectation and pupils' intellectual development.* New York: Holt, Rinehart, & Winston.

Rovee-Collier, C. (1995). Time windows in cognitive development. *Developmental Psychology, 31,* 147–169.

Rowe, M. (1974). Science, silence, and sanctions. *Science and Children, 6,* 11–13.

Rowe, M. (1986). Wait time: Slowing down may be a way of speeding up! *Journal of Teacher Education, 37,* 43–50.

Ryan, R. M., Mims, B., & Koestner, R. (1983). Relation of reward contingency and interpersonal context to intrinsic motivation: A review and test using cognitive evaluation theory. *Journal of Personality and Social Psychology, 45,* 736–750.

Sadker, D., & Sadker, M. (1985, January). Is the OK classroom OK? *Phi Delta Kappan,* 358–361.

Samuels, S. J. (2002). Reading fluency: Its development and assessment. In A. E. Farstrup & S. J. Samuels (Eds.), *What research has to say about reading instruction* (pp. 166–183). Newark, DE: International Reading Association.

Sanders, W. L., & Horn, S. P. (1994). The Tennessee value-added assessment system (TVAAS): Mixed-model methodology in educational assessment. *Journal of Personnel Evaluation in Education, 8,* 299–311.

Sanders, W. L., & Horn, S. P. (1998). Research findings for the Tennessee value-added assessment system (TVAAS) database: Implications for educational evaluation and research. *Journal of Personnel Evaluation in Education, 12*(3), 247–256.

Sanders, W. L., & Rivers, J. C. (1996, November). *Cumulative and residual effects of teachers on future student achievement.* Knoxville: University of Tennessee Value Added Assessment System.

Sanders, W. L., Wright, S. P., & Horn, S. P. (1997). Teacher and classroom context effects on student achievement: Implications for teacher evaluation. *Journal of Personnel Evaluations in Education, 11,* 57–67.

Sarler, C. (1992, February 17). Stiffen your lips, Yanks. *Newsweek, 52.*

Schunk, D. H., & Meece, J. L. (Eds.). (1992). *Student perceptions in the classroom.* Hillsdale, NJ: Erlbaum.

Seymour, D., & Seymour, T. (1992). *America's best classrooms: How award-winning teachers are shaping our culture's future.* Princeton, NJ: Peterson's Guides.

Shabani, D. B., & Carr, J. E. (2004). An evaluation of response cards as an adjunct to standard instruction in university classrooms: A systematic replication and extension. *North American Journal of Psychology, 6,* 85–100.

Sidman, M. (2000). *Coercion and its fallout* (Rev. ed.). Boston: Authors Cooperative.

Sindelar, P. T., Monda, L. E., & O'Shea, L. J. (1990). Effects of repeated readings on instructional and mastery-learning readers. *Journal of Educational Research, 83,* 220–226.

Skinner, B. F. (1958). Teaching machines. *Science, 128,* 969–977. Reprinted in B. F. Skinner (1968), *The technology of teaching* (pp. 29–58). Englewood Cliffs, NJ: Prentice-Hall.

Skinner, B. F. (1968). *The technology of teaching.* Englewood Cliffs, NJ: Prentice-Hall.

Slavin, R. E. (1983). *Cooperative learning.* New York: Longman.

Slavin, R. E. (1994). *A practical guide to cooperative learning.* Boston: Allyn & Bacon.

Smith, B. O. (1985, June). Research bases for teacher education. *Phi Delta Kappan,* 685–690.

Smith, E., Gay, S. D., Dove, H., Kircher, L., & Heras, H. (1997). Frequency and effects of teachers voice problems. *Journal of Voice, 11*(1), 81–87.

Smutny, J. F. (2003). *Differential instruction.* Bloomington, IN: PDK Education Foundation.

Soar, R. S., & Soar, R. M. (1979). Emotional climate and management. In P. Peterson & H. Walberg (Eds.), *Research on teaching: Concepts, findings, and implications.* Berkeley, CA: McCutchan.

Staats, A. W., & Butterfield, W. H. (1965). Treatment of nonreading in a culturally deprived juvenile delinquent: An application of reinforcement principles. *Child Development, 36,* 925–942.

Stahl, S. A. (2004). What do we know about fluency? Findings of the National Reading Panel. In P. McCardle & V. Chabra (Eds.), *The voice of evidence in reading research* (pp. 187–211). Baltimore: Paul H. Brookes.

Sternberg, R. E. (2003). Attending to teacher attire. *School Administrator, 60*(2), 38–44, 46.

Stevens, R. J., & Duffy, J. R. (2000). Elementary education. In A. E. Kazdin (Ed.), *Encyclopedia of psychology* (vol. 3, pp. 157–161). Washington, DC: American Psychological Association & Oxford University Press.

Stevenson, H. (1992, December). Learning from Asian schools. *Scientific American,* 70–76.

Stevenson, H. W., & Stigler, J. W. (1994). *The learning gap: Why our schools are failing and what we can learn from Japanese and Chinese education.* New York: Simon & Schuster.

Sulzer-Azaroff, B., & Mayer, G. R. (1977). *Applying behavior analysis procedures with children and youth.* New York: Holt.

Tattersall, I. (2002). *The monkey in the mirror.* New York: Harcourt.

Taylor, I., & O'Reilly, M. (1997). Toward a functional analysis of private verbal self regulation. *Journal of Applied Behavior Analysis, 30,* 43–58.

Tennyson, R. D., Wooley, F. R., & Merrill, M. D. (1972). Exemplar and non-exemplar variables which produce correct concept classification behavior and specified classification errors. *Journal of Educational Psychology, 63,* 144–152.

Thomas, D. R., Becker, W. C., & Armstrong, M. (1968). Production and elimination of disruptive behavior by systematically varying teacher behavior. *Journal of Applied Behavior Analysis, 1,* 33–45.

Thorndike, E. L. (1927). The law of effect. *American Journal of Psychology, 39,* 212–222.

Thorndike, E. L. (1931/1966). *Human learning.* Cambridge, MA: MIT Press.

Travers, R. M. W., Van Wagenen, R. K., Haygood, D. H., & McCormick, M. (1964). Learning as a consequence of the learner's task involvement under different conditions of feedback. *Journal of Educational Psychology, 55,* 167–173.

Trowbridge, M. H., & Cason, H. (1932). An experimental study of Thorndike's theory of learning. *Journal of General Psychology, 7,* 245–258.

Trujillo, C. (1986). A comparative examination of classroom interactions between professors and minority and nonminority college students. *American Educational Research Journal, 23,* 629–642.

Turner, J. C., Midgley, C., Meyer, D. K., Gheen, M., Anderman, E. M., & Kang, Y. (2002). The classroom environment and students' reports of avoidance strategies in mathematics: A multimethod study. *Journal of Educational Psychology, 94*(1), 88–106.

Vasta, R., & Stirpe, L. A. (1979). Reinforcement effects on three measures of children's interest in math. *Behavior Modification, 3,* 223–244.

Walberg, H. J. (1984, May). Improving the productivity of America's schools. *Educational Leadership,* 19–27.

Whimbey, A. (1980). *Intelligence can be taught.* New York: Dutton.

Whimbey, A., & Lochhead, J. (1999). *Problem solving and comprehension.* New York: LEA.

Wilson, S. M. (1990, November). The secret garden of teacher education. *Phi Delta Kappan,* 204–209.

Wink, L. W. (1996, Fall). Students want more discipline, disruptive classmates out. *American Educator,* 12–14.

Wolfe, D. (1951). Training. In S. S. Stevens (Ed.), *Handbook of experimental psychology.* New York: John Wiley & Sons.

Woodworth, R. S. (1938). *Experimental psychology.* New York: Holt.

Wright, J., & Cleary, K. S. (2006). Kids in the tutor seat: Building schools' capacity to help struggling readers through a cross-age peer-tutoring program. *Psychology in the Schools, 43,* 99–107.

Yurick, A. L., Robinson, P. D., Cartledge, G., Lo, Y., & Evans, T. L. (2006). Using peer-mediated repeated readings as a fluency-building activity for urban learners. *Education and Treatment of Children, 29,* 469–493.

Zeelenberg, M., Inman, J. J., & Pieters, R. G. M. (2001). What do we do when decisions go awry: Behavioral consequences of experienced regret. In E. U. Weber, J. Baron, & G. Loomes (Eds.), *Conflict and trade-offs in decision making* (pp. 136–155). Cambridge, UK: Cambridge University Press.

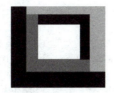

Index